Praise for *Raise Them Up*

In the beginning, God's Word was the force that caused cells to converge and molecules to amass. It called into being what had never existed before. His Word has not changed. It has not lost its power. When God fills a parent's heart with His Word and then, out of the overflow of the heart, prayer flows, the very same earth-changing power is released into the lives of our children. His in-the-beginning Word is also His right-now Word. *Raise Them Up* supplies the encouragement and inspiration, as well as practical guidance, for praying the power of God's Word into the circumstances of earth.

—**Jennifer Kennedy Dean,** executive director of The Praying Life Foundation, author of *Live a Praying Life*® and numerous books and Bible studies

I have long been an advocate for pursuing a strong parent-child relationship through growing closer to God and one another. *Raise Them Up* helps you do that. You'll have the opportunity to pray for a child's peace, relationships, purity, and boldness in faith. Partnering with God in prayer for your child's life helps you see His plans unfold for them.

—**Dannah Gresh,** founder of True Girl, author of *A Mom's Guide to Lies Girls Believe*

Raise Them Up is a vital, must-read and *do* book for every parent. Praying scriptures over your children is the key to raising up leaders. I know—I pray the Word over my family and have watched God raise up all of my children to overcome obstacles to become adults of faith who see God's power, peace, and provision in their daily lives, their own families, and in their ministry to others.

—**Pam Farrel,** international speaker, bestselling author of 46 books including *10 Best Decisions a Parent Can Make*

Raise Them Up will supercharge your prayer life! As a parent, I love this practical book because it gives me a plan to pray Scripture over my children. What could be more important? Pray through these pages and expect God to transform your home by the power of the Holy Spirit. You'll be eternally glad you did!

—**Arlene Pellicane,** speaker, author of *Parents Rising* and *Value What's Right*

Are you concerned for the spiritual, mental, emotional, and physical welfare of your children? Then *Raise Them Up* is the book for you. Sally Burke, president of Moms in Prayer, and Cyndie Claypool de Neve not only testify to the power of prayer but equip every parent with the powerful biblical tools to pray effectively. I can't wait to get this book into the hands of every Christian parent I know!

—**Cheryl Brodersen,** host of *Living Grace* on CalvaryChapel.com, speaker, author of *A Woman's Battle for Grace*

As a mother of three on this journey of parenting, praying, and patience, I joyfully endorse *Raise Them Up*! This book is a beautiful tool to encourage our souls to press on and continue to ask, seek, and knock for the lives of our children. My prayer is that we will not give up and that no matter the circumstances, we will continue to proclaim God's goodness and purpose over the lives of our children.

—**Wendy Palau,** National Prayer Team, Luis Palau Association

If you have ever felt led to pray for your kids but couldn't find the right words, *Raise Them Up* is the practical tool you have been looking for. It is a clarion call for parents to lean in to the power of prayer for raising thriving kids who become faith-filled adults. This book is inspiring, challenging, and filled with deep wisdom about what your kids need most from you. You'll refer to it again and again.

—**Mandy Arioto,** president and CEO of MOPS International

Raise Them Up

SALLY BURKE AND
CYNDIE CLAYPOOL DE NEVE

HARVEST HOUSE PUBLISHERS
EUGENE, OREGON

Cover design by Kara Klontz Design

Cover photos © maxim ibragimov, Mybona, Pranch, Seohwa Kim / Shutterstock

Published in association with William K. Jensen Literary Agency, 119 Bampton Court, Eugene, Oregon 97404.

Raise Them Up
Copyright © 2019 by Sally Burke and Cyndie Claypool de Neve
Published by Harvest House Publishers
Eugene, Oregon 97408
www.harvesthousepublishers.com

ISBN 978-0-7369-6979-6 (Trade)
ISBN 978-0-7369-6980-2 (eBook)

Library of Congress Cataloging-in-Publication Data

Names: Burke, Sally (President of Moms in Prayer International), author. | De Neve, Cyndie Claypool, author.
Title: Raise them up / Sally Burke and Cyndie Claypool de Neve.
Description: Eugene, Oregon : Harvest House Publishers, [2019] |
Identifiers: LCCN 2019011806 (print) | LCCN 2019014705 (ebook) | ISBN 9780736969802 (ebook) | ISBN 9780736969796 (pbk.)
Subjects: LCSH: Parents--Religious life. | Prayer--Christianity.
Classification: LCC BV4529 (ebook) | LCC BV4529 .B86 2019 (print) | DDC 242/.6431--dc23
LC record available at https://lccn.loc.gov/2019011806

Printed in the United States of America

19 20 21 22 23 24 25 26 27 / BP-RD / 10 9 8 7 6 5 4 3 2 1

Contents

Part III: Encouraging the Legacy of Prayer

This book is dedicated to every parent whose heart has ached for their child, who has wondered where they can turn for help, who has cried out to God, not knowing if He hears. We pray this book will help you pray the big, bold scripture prayers for your children—no matter if they're in diapers, in school, or settled into adulthood—knowing that God always cares and always hears the cry of our heart.

This is our prayer for you as you cry out to the Lord on behalf of your children:

> *May the LORD answer you when you are in distress;*
> *may the name of the God of Jacob protect you.*
> *May he send you help from the sanctuary*
> *and grant you support...*
> *May he give you the desire of your heart*
> *and make all your plans succeed.*
> *May we shout for joy over your victory*
> *and lift up our banners in the name of our God.*

PSALM 20:1-2,4-5

Foreword

by **Fern Nichols,**
Founder of Moms in Prayer International

I believe the greatest impact a mom can have in the life of her child is through prayer. Therefore, the truth of James 5:16 is noteworthy: "The prayer of a righteous person is powerful and effective." It is the child of God who prays with a pure heart whose prayer exercises force. Yes, prayer has power! It creates change and produces an impact. This book will help you pray with power and with confidence. God is just waiting for you to ask so that He can bring His power to bear.

You probably have heard it said that God's Word is an offensive weapon that destroys the enemy's strategies. Well, that's true. We can run at the enemy and overpower him with the Word.

> Jesus said to him, "Away from me, Satan! For it is written: 'Worship the Lord your God, and serve him only'" (Matthew 4:10).

This is what Jesus said when tempted by Satan. What a model for us to follow, holding up the Word of God in the face of the enemy and saying with faith and boldness, "It is written!" And then we say with the psalmist, "My eyes strain to see your rescue, to see the truth of your promise fulfilled" (Psalm 119:123 NLT).

Praying God's Word is praying God's heart and His will. In believing this, you turn your timid prayers into mighty, believing, unwavering-faith prayers. God's Word is God-breathed, alive, living, inerrant, active, and powerful. It's His voice that speaks into the now.

Personalizing a scripture by inserting a child's name into the text has opened the eyes of moms to how powerful and personal the Word really is. One mom stated, "I find great peace in knowing that I can depend on the constant and unchangeable promises of God." Week after week, moms leave their Moms in Prayer group with hope and victory. Why? Because they have learned to trust that God is who He says He is, and He will do what He says He will do. All of His promises are backed by the honor of His name. These truths carry them throughout the week as they seek God on behalf of their children and schools. They are in tiptoe anticipation to see the promises fulfilled.

························

Praying God's Word is praying God's heart and His will. In believing this, you turn your timid prayers into mighty, believing, unwavering-faith prayers.

························

The topical scripture prayers in this book are faith building. They will give you the assurance that you are praying God's heart and the desire to search God's Word for yourself. As you read the testimonies woven throughout the book, you will be drawn into a deeper relationship with your Lord and inspired to pray more, trust more, and walk more closely with your heavenly Father. You'll know beyond the shadow of a doubt that He hears your cries and will answer.

Raise Them Up is a life-changing book you will refer to often because it leads you to a deeper realization that as you partner with Christ and lift up your child and life in the name of Jesus, history will change.

This is a resource that shouts, "With God nothing is impossible!"

Part I

A Lifeline for Every Parent: Prayer

Experiencing the Power of Prayer in Our Lives

Sally Burke,
President of Moms in Prayer International

And yet God...

I have personally seen how scriptural prayer has brought great hope to the one praying, and revival, spiritual awakening, purpose, and life to the one who is prayed for. I have seen this truth happen all over the world in the most hopeless and impossible situations.

True intercession is standing in the gap on behalf of another, seeking the fullness of God's will for that person. Only God truly knows the purposes and plans He created a person for. He tells us they are for good and to give a future and hope (Jeremiah 29:11). He does not want anyone to perish but everyone to come to repentance (2 Peter 3:9).

God's Word is His will. And as you pray His Word on behalf of another, you will unleash His power to do His will. His Word is powerful. God formed all things by His creative word and continues to govern all things by the power of His Word. Prayer using God's Word is an unstoppable force. God will reach out and touch that person's life.

You will be blessed as well.

As you pray His Word, He moves through you, transforming your heart and mind in Christ Jesus, giving you exceeding hope.

The one interceding and the one prayed for will be equally blessed by God's hand and Word. His Word is crucially important. Hebrews 4:12 says, "For the word of God is alive and active. Sharper than any double-edged sword, it penetrates even to dividing soul and spirit, joints and marrow; it judges the thoughts and attitudes of the heart."

We see things around us and feel hopeless to change the course of history. God sees things eternally and looks for someone willing to stand in the gap, so He can change the course of *His* story (Eze-kiel 22). God's Word always fulfills His purposes (Isaiah 55). Just as Jesus fulfilled His great destiny, God desires that all people fulfill the great calling He has for them. As Jesus says in Matthew 19:26, "With God all things are possible."

God's Word reaches higher than you can ever imagine and goes deeper than you could ask, bringing forth salvation, completion, peace, joy, truth, and glory to God. Jesus says in John 15:7-8, "If you remain in me and my words remain in you, ask whatever you wish, and it will be done for you. This is to my Father's glory, that you bear much fruit, showing yourselves to be my disciples."

· ·

We see things around us and feel hopeless to change the course of history. God sees things eternally and looks for someone willing to stand in the gap, so He can change the course of His story

· ·

Cyndie is a dear friend, sister, prayer warrior, and partner in the books *Unshaken, Unshaken Study Guide, Start with Praise,* and now this one, *Raise Them Up.* I had the privilege of meeting Cyn-die several years ago. We worked together at Moms in Prayer Inter-national when she was our Director of Communications. Her love for God, His Word, prayer, and others has impacted our ministry and many for Christ. When God placed upon my heart the desire to share what He is doing as women gather together to pray, I knew she would be the one I would partner with.

Together, Cyndie and I share this book with anticipation of its impact on you and the people you care about. When we embark on the adventure of intercessory prayer, the power of the Lord and His Word manifests in our life and the lives of those we lift up. Throughout this journey, we will share inspiring stories from women who have witnessed this power and impact as they raise up their children and this generation through prayer.

....

God's Word reaches higher than you can ever imagine and goes deeper than you could ask.

....

As we pray God's Word over one another, we will see that which is eternal and bring hope and life to those around us. "For everything that was written in the past was written to teach us, so that through the endurance taught in the Scriptures and the encouragement they provide we might have hope" (Romans 15:4).

Our prayer for you and those you pray for:

*May the God of hope fill you with all joy and peace
as you trust in him, so that you may overflow
with hope by the power of the Holy Spirit.*

Romans 15:13

1

The Four Steps of Prayer

Do not be anxious about anything, but in every situation, by
prayer and petition, with thanksgiving, present your requests to
God. And the peace of God, which transcends all understanding,
will guard your hearts and your minds in Christ Jesus.

PHILIPPIANS 4:6-7

Parenting is not for the faint of heart. Almost no other role
requires more choices and decisions that have such a profound,
long-lasting impact.

And as stressful as parenting can be when we are standing right
beside our son or daughter, it becomes more stressful when they are
not in our presence—no matter how old the child is! The fear this
triggers in a parent's spirit is the reason we're witnessing the rise of
technology designed to help us check in on our kids—from nanny
cams to tracking devices and apps. Nowadays, cell phones and text
messaging make it easier to get hold of our kids. But if we don't hear
back, we can imagine the worst! Even camps have been pressured
into posting pictures of campers so parents can see their kids are
alive and well.

But even with all these tools, the reality is that we can never know
exactly where our child is and what they are doing. Thankfully, there
is Someone who always knows where our children are. Our heavenly
Father is sovereign. He is all-seeing and all-knowing. Proverbs 15:3
reminds us, "The eyes of the LORD are everywhere, keeping watch

on the wicked and the good." We can relax, knowing that the One who loves us also loves our children.

How does this make you feel? If you have a relationship with Christ, then you probably feel a sense of peace, knowing your child is in good hands. That's why Moms in Prayer starts each prayer time with praise and then moves toward closing with intercession. By first focusing on God's loving, caring, compassionate, purposeful, and wise characteristics, we are reminded that even when we aren't in control, we can trust the One who is.

....

The One who loves us also loves our children.

....

My (Cyndie's) friend Patty Goh recently texted me as she was packing up her daughter for her freshman year at a public university. She wrote:

> I woke up in the morning with anxiety, fearing my children would suffer because of my parenting style. But God gave me 1 Peter 5:7 when I opened up the *Daily Bread* devotion: "Cast all your anxiety on Him because He cares for you." At that moment I remembered that God knows what I've been through. He wants me not to worry, but to keep praying. He will take care of my precious children.

That is the beauty of prayer, especially scripture prayer: We can hand over all our worries, fears, and anxieties to God, and He promises in Philippians 4:6-7 that He will replace all our angst with His inexplicable peace.

Lord, help _____ cast all his/her anxieties
on You because You care for him/her.

FROM 1 PETER 5:7

Before we dive into praying scriptures for our children and specific parts of their lives, let's first look at the four steps of prayer. This is not the only way to pray, but it is an effective way to refocus our minds and align our prayers with Christ. Whether you're frustrated with a stubborn toddler, fearful for a school-age student who's struggling to make friends, worried about a teenager's choices, or concerned your adult child hasn't reached out to you in weeks, starting your prayer time with praise and moving to confession and thanksgiving refocuses our minds on how big God is, not on how big the problem seems to be. Then we move to praying for another, which is called intercession. Resting in God's character and faithfulness, we can lift up a child with confidence and hope.

Praise

When we start by praising God, we move our focus from our problem to the Problem-solver, from the chaos to the One who calms the storms, from the unknowns to the One who is all-knowing. Read Psalm 103 and focus on the attributes and characteristics of the Almighty.

Psalm 103:1-13

> Praise the LORD, my soul;
>   all my inmost being, praise his holy name.
> Praise the LORD, my soul,
>   and forget not all his benefits—
> who forgives all your sins
> and heals all your diseases,
> who redeems your life from the pit
>   and crowns you with love and compassion,
> who satisfies your desires with good things
>   so that your youth is renewed like the eagle's.
> The LORD works righteousness
>   and justice for all the oppressed.

> He made known his ways to Moses,
>   his deeds to the people of Israel:
> The LORD is compassionate and gracious,
>   slow to anger, abounding in love.
> He will not always accuse,
>   nor will he harbor his anger forever;
> he does not treat us as our sins deserve
> or repay us according to our iniquities.
> For as high as the heavens are above the earth,
> so great is his love for those who fear him;
> as far as the east is from the west,
>   so far has he removed our transgressions from us.
> As a father has compassion on his children,
>   so the LORD has compassion on those who fear him.

How do you feel after focusing on God our Father? If you started this chapter with a concern weighing heavy on your heart, did this passage have an impact on how you felt? What's one attribute of God that you want to praise Him for? If you're not sure, look back through these verses and pick one to lift up. Maybe today you want to praise the Lord for His compassion, His forgiveness of all your sins, His slowness to anger, or His overflowing love for you. Spend a few minutes praising the Lord.

Confession

The second step of prayer, confession, allows us to get right with the Lord so we are prepared as a holy vessel to pray according to God's will. Do you want powerful and effective prayers? The key is to cleanse your heart before the Lord, to align your requests with His. James 5:16 says, "The prayer of a righteous person is powerful and effective." Read John 15:7-12:

> If you remain in me and my words remain in you, ask whatever you wish, and it will be done for you. This is to my Father's glory, that you bear much fruit, showing

yourselves to be my disciples. As the Father has loved me, so have I loved you. Now remain in my love. If you keep my commands, you will remain in my love, just as I have kept my Father's commands and remain in his love. I have told you this so that my joy may be in you and that your joy may be complete.

The key to the promise in verse 7 is found in verses 9 and 10: When we remain in God's love by keeping His commands, then God will do whatever we ask in prayer. But can we, as mere humans, live in God's commands all day, every day? No. And that's the beauty of confession. First John 1:9 assures us, "If we confess our sins, he is faithful and just and will forgive us our sins and purify us from all unrighteousness." And when we confess, we realign our will with His will to better pray the will of the Lord.

Thanksgiving

Many who study science are now realizing what men and women of God have known forever: Giving thanks has a powerful impact on our minds. But, of course, the One who created our minds already knew the power of being thankful, which is why He commands it: "Give thanks in all circumstances; for this is God's will for you in Christ Jesus" (1 Thessalonians 5:18). When we begin to focus on our blessings and the prayers God has answered, it reminds us to keep trusting Him and keep praying and keep persevering.

Intercession

James 4:2 tells us, "You do not have because you do not ask God." We can have a powerful impact on others' lives through intercessory prayer, by standing in the gap for them, asking the Lord to intervene in a powerful way. And that's exactly what this book is about. How do we know for certain what God's will for someone's life is? By praying Scripture!

Specifically, we'll look at verses that can be prayed for any child in your life. Maybe you're a coach or schoolteacher or youth worker, and you want to have a greater impact in the lives of those with whom you work. Or maybe you're a parent, aunt, uncle, grandparent, or other relative who wants to pray God's blessings on the lives of those within your family. Or perhaps you don't know the names of the children in your neighborhood, but you want to pray for them.

....

How do we know for certain what God's will for someone's life is? By praying Scripture!

....

This book is set up by subjects for which to pray: Christian character, salvation, protection, freedom from addiction, their future, and many more. You can pray through the life categories in the order we present them, or you can jump around to pray scriptures based on a child's immediate needs.

At the end of each chapter is a section called Scripture Prayers. Most of these verses are formatted to make it easy to pray by providing a line where you can fill in a child's name. Feel free to use your phone to take a photo of a page of verses that are particularly meaningful for your situation. This way, when you start to fear, you can turn to prayer. If you're married, we encourage you to pray the scriptures together with your spouse. While many of the testimonies we share are from our Moms in Prayer ministry, the principles of prayer, of course, are applicable for everyone.

Beginning with a Prayer

Lord, as Psalm 103 says, we praise You for being "compassionate and gracious, slow to anger, abounding in love." We do not deserve Your love and compassion, yet You freely bestow these upon us. Forgive us for the times we worry and take matters into our own hands, forgetting that Your timing is always perfect. Lord, thank You for this journey we embark on to pray Your words over our children. Help us remember that when we begin to fear, we need to, instead, go to prayer. James 4:2 says we don't have because we don't ask. Lord, help us to remember to ask in Your powerful name and to wait on Your perfect timing, knowing that Your love and compassion extend to our child and that You promise to work all things together for Your good purpose (Romans 8:28).

2

The Power of Praying Scriptures

The grass withers and the flowers fall, but the
word of our God endures forever.

Isaiah 40:8

Prayer is the act of inviting God's presence and power into our lives, into our situations, into our world. Prayer ushers in God's will to be done here on earth as it is in heaven. It is the greatest power available to God's children, and when it is combined with God's Word, it is an unstoppable force.

Just think about the power of God's Word. God spoke the heavens and earth into being! "In the beginning God created the heavens and the earth. Now the earth was formless and empty, darkness was over the surface of the deep, and the Spirit of God was hovering over the waters. And God said, 'Let there be light,' and there was light. God saw that the light was good, and he separated the light from the darkness" (Genesis 1:1-4). God's Word went forth powerfully, accomplishing His will in creation. His will includes a mighty plan for you and those you are praying for.

His plans are greater than our plans. He asserts this in Isaiah 55:8-11:

> "For my thoughts are not your thoughts, neither are your ways my ways," declares the Lord. "As the heavens are higher than the earth, so are my ways higher than your ways and my thoughts than your thoughts. As the rain and

the snow come down from heaven, and do not return to it
without watering the earth and making it bud and flourish,
so that it yields seed for the sower and bread for the eater, so
is my word that goes out from my mouth: It will not return
to me empty but will accomplish what I desire and achieve
the purpose for which I sent it."

Don't you love the promise in this passage? His Word will accomplish what He desires and achieve His purpose. Sometimes we pray and see quick answers to prayer, like when rain falls and pools on the ground; and sometimes we pray God's Word, and it goes down deep into the ground, and years later we see what God intended as an answer for those long-lasting prayers. What we aren't able to see right away is often nourishing the soil for God's plans to bear fruit in us and our lives.

Only God truly knows the purposes for which He created each person—every child and every adult. Yes, we're created for fellowship with Him and to bring Him glory, but He also created each of His children with gifts and talents. And He created the circumstances by which to bring Him glory. When we intercede for others, we come alongside God, seeking His face and His will for their lives. We are those vessels He works through to accomplish great things on their behalf as we pray. When we pray His scriptures over them, we witness Him do "immeasurably more than all we ask or imagine" (Ephesians 3:20).

What Happens When We Pray Scripture

One year, while I (Sally) was praying for my oldest, I witnessed how God's ways are always higher than mine for my children. That year my son was on the baseball team, but he spent most of every game sitting on the bench. Of course, I thought he should be playing more. Can you relate? At each game I would pray that he would have a chance to play and hit a home run or make the winning catch. Yet, in my Moms in Prayer group, I was praying Scripture over him, like Philippians 2:14-16:

> "Do everything without grumbling or arguing, so that you may become blameless and pure, 'children of God without fault in a warped and crooked generation.' Then you will shine among them like stars in the sky as you hold firmly to the word of life. And then I will be able to boast on the day of Christ that I did not run or labor in vain."

Lord, help _____ do everything without grumbling or arguing so that he/she will become blameless and pure, a child of God without fault in a warped and crooked generation. Help _____ shine among them like stars in the sky, as he/she holds firmly to Your word of life.

FROM PHILIPPIANS 2:14-16

He never hit the home run or caught the winning catch, but my son's coach came up to me one day and asked if my son was a Christian. I replied, "Yes," and inquired why he was asking. He explained that my son did everything without complaining and grumbling and was an example to all on his team. The Lord showed me that the souls of the lost are much more important than the home runs I was praying for. God's ways are always greater than my ways. Many people have come to know Jesus through my son—and *not* because he had the highest baseball stats. Praying Scripture for him did not come back void, but my worldly desires did. "Heaven and earth will pass away, but My words will not pass away" (Matthew 24:35 NASB).

His Word is also sustaining and powerful. In Hebrews 1:3, God talks about sustaining all things by His powerful Word. "The Son is the radiance of God's glory and the exact representation of his being, sustaining all things by his powerful word."

You may not realize this, but every atom is held together by an invisible force that scientists call gluon. If you split an atom, you get atomic power. And yet God's Word is much more explosive and powerful than that.

God is waiting to unleash His power and His Word through you to bless many. Prayer ushers us into God's presence and His power. We can all praise God that He works through imperfect, fallible men and women to accomplish His will through prayer. Every answer to prayer brings glory to God! How do you know God will answer your prayers? "If you remain in me and my words in you, ask whatever you wish and it will be done for you. This is to my Father's glory, that you bear much fruit showing yourselves to be my disciples" (John 15:7-8). When we pray the mighty Word of God, we pray according to His will.

....

God is waiting to unleash His power and
His Word through you to bless many.

....

May you go forth empowered through praying Scripture over your child, impacting generations to come. May you send forth His Word in prayer to accomplish great and mighty things on behalf of your children and those around them. May your heart rejoice as His Scripture goes out through your prayers to accomplish His great will. And may you bear much fruit, showing yourself to be His disciple.

Scripture Prayers for Your Journey

I call on you, my God, for you will answer me;
turn your ear to me and hear my prayer.

PSALM 17:6

I will trust in him at all times, and pour out
my heart to him, for God is my refuge.

FROM PSALM 62:8

Listen to my words, LORD, consider my lament. Hear my
cry for help, my King and my God, for to you I pray. In
the morning, LORD, you hear my voice; in the morning
I lay my requests before you and wait expectantly.

PSALM 5:1-3

I lift up my eyes to the mountains—where does my help
come from? My help comes from the LORD, the Maker
of heaven and earth. He will not let your foot slip—he
who watches over you will not slumber; indeed, he who
watches over Israel will neither slumber nor sleep.

PSALM 121:1-4

If I had cherished sin in my heart, the LORD would
not have listened; but God has surely listened and
has heard my prayer. Praise be to God, who has not
rejected my prayer or withheld his love from me!

PSALM 66:18-20

The earnest prayer of a righteous person has
great power and produces wonderful results.

JAMES 5:16 NLT

If I remain in you and your words in me, whatever I ask
will be done for me. This is to the Father's glory, that
I bear much fruit showing myself to be a disciple.

From John 15:7-8

~

*Arise, cry out in the night, as the watches of the night
begin; pour out your heart like water in the presence of
the Lord. Lift up your hands to him for the lives of your
children, who faint from hunger at every street corner.*

Lamentations 2:19

Part II

Praying God's Word over a Child's Life

3

Praying Christ's Character into the Lives of Children

*And Solomon, my son, learn to know
the God of your ancestors intimately.
Worship and serve him with your whole heart and a willing
mind. For the LORD sees every heart and knows every
plan and thought. If you seek him, you will find him.*

1 CHRONICLES 28:9 NLT

We don't always know what's best for our kids. If it were up to us, we'd pray that our children would have perfect lives, free of health problems, stress, grief, or struggles of any kind. Yet facing difficulties and challenges is often the very thing that refines our character and shapes us into who God created us to be. That's why, before we dive into praying for specific requests, we want to encourage you to pray for the children in your life to develop Christlike character. To encourage you, we'll start with this testimony from Lisa Freyschlag.

I knew early on that I was a worrier. At 13, I worried so much about what others thought of me that I finally asked God, *"Who am I?"* At 19, I worried myself into physical anxiety over whether to drop a college class. I didn't want to be a quitter! So, how in the world could I one day become a peaceful mom who wouldn't worry every moment about her children? Moms in Prayer entered my life.

In the 1990s when my kids were in elementary school, a friend invited me to a then-named "Moms in Touch" prayer group. It became my favorite hour of every week because I entered that time and that group with varied concerns and left feeling washed over with the peace of God. I changed from a mom-worrier into a prayer warrior. I grew to know and trust God more deeply through praising a different one of His attributes each week, and I watched the power of God build godly character in our kids as we prayed specific scriptures over them together, week after week.

Fast-forward 25 years to now. The children we prayed for then are now adults who are having their own children! Recently, I pulled a dusty book off the shelf to look back at the character qualities and Scripture verses my group had prayed over our children more than 20 years ago. I felt unexpected tears coming. They turned into a full-fledged flood, and I had to pull my husband away from a project to share God's amazing revelation of answers after years of praying scriptures for our kids.

The virtues and matching scriptures that I had felt led to pray for each child seemed to have miraculously bloomed into their lives, and truly describe the adults they have become! As I read these qualities, I was overwhelmed by the evidence of God's personal touch on each of their lives.

For my oldest daughter—vow-keeper, strong conviction, faith, purity, opportunity (she grasped many with great leadership!), available to God, knowing His goodness, and my favorite: *laughter*. She learned to laugh through her perfectionism as she grew in God's freedom. The verse was Proverbs 15:15 (NKJV), "He who is of a merry heart has a continual feast."

For my youngest daughter—authentic, fair, original (oh yes, she is!), good choices (even when she said she was about to rebel!), courage, and my favorite: *treasure hunter*. She joyously searches for the best and finds it in God. The verse was Psalm 119:162 (NKJV), "I rejoice at Your word as one who finds great treasure."

For my only son—truthful, full of creativity, honors others, heart for missions, strong character, and, since he is now in seminary, my heart stood still when I read the final attribute prayed over him: *kingdom builder*. And that's where God has his heart now, shepherding others in building God's kingdom. The verses were Luke 12:32,34 (NKJV): "Do not fear...for it is your Father's good pleasure to give you the kingdom...For where your treasure is, there your heart will be also."

It's no wonder the tears came. Now I can say with assurance and wonder, "Thank You, God, for specific answers to prayer and for building *Your* character into our children as we prayed scripture prayers over them from decades ago to this very day."

· ·

Facing difficulties and challenges is often the very thing that refines our character and shapes us into who God created us to be.

· ·

When we pray scripture prayers for our child to have Christ's character, we are asking God to fill our child with godly attributes so God's will can be done in their lives. You will discover, just as Lisa did, that not one prayer is wasted. You might consider keeping a record of your specific prayers for your child or children so that you, too, can remember God's faithfulness and praise Him for being a part of your child's life from beginning to end.

Scripture Prayers for Christlike Character

The Bible is filled with wonderful scriptures to pray over our children as they grow to be like Christ. Most of the Scripture Prayer sections throughout this book will provide verses that are just one or two sentences long, like the first couple below. However, for this section, we offer some longer Bible passages to really pour out the power of Christ over the children for whom you pray. Each of these is formatted so it can be personalized by adding in a child's name.

Lord, help _____ be a man/woman after Your own heart and do everything You want him/her to do.

FROM ACTS 13:22

I pray _____ will acknowledge You, God the Father, and serve You with wholehearted devotion and a willing mind, for You, Lord, search every heart and understand every desire and every thought.

FROM 1 CHRONICLES 28:9

Help _____ be strong and very courageous, to be careful to obey all the law and not to turn from it to the right or to the left, that _____ may be successful wherever he/she goes. Impassion _____ to keep this Book of the Law always on his/her lips; to meditate on it day and night, so that he/she will be careful to do everything written in it. Then _____ will be prosperous and successful. Help him/her to remember Your command to be strong and courageous, to not be afraid. Help him/her to not be discouraged, for You, Lord, will be with _____ wherever he/she goes.

FROM JOSHUA 1:7-9

Lord, I pray that _____ will live out the fruit of the Spirit in his/her life. Empower him/her to be filled with Your love, joy, peace, forbearance, kindness, goodness, faithfulness, gentleness and self-control. Help _____ desire to belong to You, Christ Jesus, and crucify his/her flesh with its passions and desires. Remind _____ daily that since we live by the Spirit, we should keep in step with the Spirit. Help him/her to not become conceited, provoking and envying others.

FROM GALATIANS 5:22-26

Lord, help _____ walk blamelessly in You, to do what is righteous, to speak the truth from his/her heart, to utter no slander, to do no wrong to a neighbor, to cast no slur on others, to honor those who fear the Lord, to keep an oath even when it hurts without changing his/her mind, to lend money to the poor without interest, and not to accept a bribe against the innocent. Empower _____ to do these things and never be shaken.

FROM PSALM 15:2-5

Because of Your great love for _____, Lord, I pray You, who are rich in mercy, will make _____ alive with Christ even though he/she may be dead in transgressions. It is by grace we have been saved. And You raised us up with Christ and seated us with Him in the heavenly realms in Christ Jesus, in order that in the coming ages You might show the incomparable riches of Your grace, expressed in Your kindness to us in Christ Jesus. For it is by grace _____ has been saved, through faith—and this is not from himself/herself, it is the gift of God—not by works, so that no one can boast. Lord, I pray that _____ will know that he/she is God's handiwork, created in Christ Jesus to do good works, which God prepared in advance for him/her to do.

FROM EPHESIANS 2:4-10

Lord, I cry out on behalf of _____ that he/she

will be raised with Christ and set his/her heart on things
above, where Christ is, seated at the right hand of God.
Help _____ set his/her mind on things above,
not on earthly things…I pray _____ will put to
death whatever belongs to his/her earthly nature: sexual
immorality, impurity, lust, evil desires and greed, which
is idolatry…Help _____ also rid himself/herself
of such things as anger, rage, malice, slander, and filthy
language. And help him/her to not lie. May he/she be
passionate about taking off his/her old self with all its
old practices and putting on the new self, which is being
renewed in knowledge in the image of the Creator. I
pray that _____'s heart desire is that Christ is all
and is in all. May _____ know he/she is holy and
dearly loved by God. Help him/her clothe himself/herself
with compassion, kindness, humility, gentleness, and
patience. May he/she bear with others and forgive others.
If _____ has a grievance against someone, help him/
her to forgive as You have forgiven him/her. And over all
these virtues help _____ put on love, which binds
us all together in perfect unity. I also pray that _____
will devote himself/herself to prayer, being watchful
and thankful…Help _____ proclaim the gospel
clearly and be wise in the way he/she acts toward outsiders,
making the most of every opportunity. Let _____'s
conversation be always full of grace, seasoned with salt,
so that he/she may know how to answer everyone.

FROM COLOSSIANS 3:1-14; 4:2-6

Lord, You tell us to keep reminding God's people of the
following things: Warn _____ against quarreling
about words; it is of no value, and only ruins those who
listen. Help _____ do his/her best to present
himself/herself to You as one approved, a worker who
does not need to be ashamed and who correctly handles
the word of truth. Remind _____ to avoid godless

chatter, because those who indulge in it will become more and more ungodly…Empower _____ to flee the evil desires of youth and pursue righteousness, faith, love and peace, along with those who call on the Lord out of a pure heart. May he/she not have anything to do with foolish and stupid arguments, because they produce quarrels. And the Lord's servant must not be quarrelsome but must be kind to everyone, able to teach, not resentful. Help _____ gently instruct opponents in the hope that God will grant them repentance, leading them to a knowledge of the truth, and that they will come to their senses and escape from the trap of the devil, who has taken them captive to do his will.

FROM 2 TIMOTHY 2:14-16,22-26

Let the peace of Christ rule in your hearts, since as members of one body you were called to peace. And be thankful. Let the message of Christ dwell among you richly as you teach and admonish one another with all wisdom through psalms, hymns, and songs from the Spirit, singing to God with gratitude in your hearts. And whatever you do, whether in word or deed, do it all in the name of the Lord Jesus, giving thanks to God the Father through him.

COLOSSIANS 3:15-17

4

Praying Salvation for Children

To open their eyes and turn them from darkness to light,
and from the power of Satan to God, so that they
may receive forgiveness of sins and a place among
those who are sanctified by faith in me.

ACTS 26:18

Nicole Jiles was in fifth grade when she first heard about Jesus at a little Bible class held in a trailer near her school. However, since her family didn't attend church, it wasn't until she was 15 years old that she heard the clear presentation of the gospel and gave her heart to the Lord. A few months later, she moved and began attending church regularly. After that, she prayed desperately that her two sisters and mom would give their hearts to the Lord. Over and over she'd pray:

"Lord, You say in 2 Peter 3:9 that You are 'not wanting anyone to perish, but everyone to come to repentance.' Please, help my sisters and mom come to know You. Don't let them perish but to come to repentance in You."

One by one, they each came to Christ. And not only her sisters, but eventually their spouses and their children. In God's perfect timing, He answered in Ephesians 3:20 style, in ways that were more than all she had asked or imagined.

Her mom had been married five times before she finally accepted Christ as her personal Savior, and then married a godly man. Nicole's mom recently passed away, but Nicole is comforted knowing that she will see her again.

What a great reminder that we all need to be praying for our unsaved loved ones—no matter the circumstances. Second Peter 3:9 reminds us to be persistent in our prayers: "The Lord is not slow in keeping his promise, as some understand slowness. Instead he is patient with you, not wanting anyone to perish, but everyone to come to repentance."

My (Cyndie's) dad grew up as a self-described "hoodlum." In fact, when he was a young teen, to get my mom's attention, he lit on fire the pile of leaves beneath her bedroom window. What we discovered many years later is that my dad was on the "cradle roll" of a local church, and faithful prayer warriors had been interceding for him. Boy, did he need it! After dropping out of high school and joining the Marines, he showed up in his uniform to the soda shop where my mom was sitting with her friend. As my mom tells the story, she took one look at him in his uniform and fell in love. Soon, the two teens were married.

Six children later, we were stationed in the very hot and windy 29 Palms in California, and my dad finally ended up going to church—thanks to the air conditioner inside the building. My two oldest sisters had started most of us kids going to Sunday school when we lived in Oceanside, but the desert church was too far to walk. My dad ended up driving us. He had originally planned to wait for us in the parking lot each time, but the heat proved to be too much. Enticed by the air conditioner, he went inside and sat in the back pew. It was in that church that he heard the gospel and came to Christ with a wholehearted transformation. Over the years, he faithfully led youth programs and church tech teams up until God called him home. I firmly believe that those cradle roll prayers guided my dad's path toward his eventual salvation—and the salvation of the many lives he impacted.

It is never too early to pray for a child to come to Christ. You might never witness the path along which God will take that life to answer the prayer of salvation in His perfect timing. My dad's name was just one of several on that list of prayed-for babies. Those praying might not have even known him or his family well. Yet they prayed. And those prayers impacted not just one man but his entire family—and each person that we have had the privilege of impacting for Christ.

For which child is God calling you to pray to have a life-transforming relationship with Christ? Maybe it's the neighbor with the newborn baby, or the mom who walks her kids to school every morning, pushing the youngest in a stroller. Or maybe it's your child or grandchild or relative. At the end of this chapter, we provide the opportunity for you to pray for this child by placing his/her name within the scripture prayers for salvation.

For which child is God calling you to pray to have a life-transforming relationship with Christ?

God Is Not Slow in Keeping His Promise

We recently received a testimony from a mom in South America.

> Something happened to me when I turned 40 years of age: The Lord revealed Himself to me and showed me my sins. I confronted my reality and fell on my knees before Him. God forgave and provided a new opportunity in my life. I began to experience a new life. I also started to pray for my son.
>
> About three years ago he was diagnosed with the HIV virus but was treated early, and as of today the results are negative.

However, he has to take a medication for the rest of his life. Last year I learned about the Moms in Prayer ministry, and I sensed the Lord's calling for me to pray for my son in a very different way. I prayed for the Lord to bring my son back to the way of the Lord. I have immersed myself in the ministry, so I may help other mothers to pray.

But the most important thing and the reason for this note is that last night my son, who lives in Buenos Aires...went to an evangelical church. He sensed the Lord's presence and forgiveness in his life. Never before have I heard my son so sure of himself and with so much joy. My heart is overflowing with joy and thanksgiving to my Lord. I have renewed strength to continue to pray.

Scripture Prayers for the Unsaved

God, You so loved _____ that You gave Your one
and only Son, for him/her. Help _____ believe
in You so he/she will not perish but have eternal life.

FROM JOHN 3:16

Lord, we thank You that You are not slow in
keeping Your promise, as some understand
slowness. Instead, You are patient with us. You do
not want anyone to perish, but everyone to come to
repentance. Lord, I pray that _____ will
come to repentance in Your perfect timing.

FROM 2 PETER 3:9

Lord, since the wages of sin is death, help _____
accept Your free gift of eternal life in Christ Jesus our Lord.

FROM ROMANS 6:23 NASB

Help _____ trust in Your unfailing love;
may his/her heart rejoice in Your salvation.

FROM PSALM 13:5

Lord, I pray _____ will declare with his/her
mouth "Jesus is Lord," and believe in his/her heart that You
raised Jesus from the dead, so _____ will be saved.

FROM ROMANS 10:9

Open _____'s eyes and turn him/her from
darkness to light, and from the power of Satan to God,
so that _____ may receive forgiveness of sins and
a place among those who are sanctified by faith in You.

FROM ACTS 26:18

Give _____ an undivided heart and put a new

spirit in him/her; remove from _____ a heart of
stone and give him/her a heart of flesh. Then he/she will
follow Your decrees and be careful to keep Your laws;
_____ will be Yours, and You will be his/her God.

FROM EZEKIEL 11:19-20

Show _____ Your unfailing love, Lord,
and grant him/her Your salvation.

FROM PSALM 85:7

~

The LORD is my strength and my defense; he has
become my salvation. He is my God, and I will praise
him, my father's God, and I will exalt him.

EXODUS 15:2

5

Praying for Schoolwork

We continually ask God to fill you with the knowledge
of his will through all the wisdom and understanding
that the Spirit gives, so that you may live a life worthy of
the Lord and please him in every way: bearing fruit in
every good work, growing in the knowledge of God.

COLOSSIANS 1:9-10

When I (Cyndie) was working for Moms in Prayer, I asked a coworker to pray for my son's high school math grade. I just wanted him to pass, as math was proving to be his Achilles' heel academically. But what did my friend do? She prayed he'd get an A! I'm not sure I hid my giggle as she asked God for what was nothing short of a miracle. But guess what happened? He changed math classes to a computerized math with an amazingly encouraging teacher. And guess what grade he received? Yes, an A! Now, I shouldn't be surprised, because God is capable of doing "more than all we ask or imagine" (Ephesians 3:20). But, boy, did that remind me to pray the big prayers academically, as well as for their character.

Of course, God doesn't always answer our prayers for our children's grades, as He truly cares more about their character than their comfort. But sometimes He knows our kids need that extra reminder of His grace. My son, Elliott, struggled with dyslexia from a young age, and schoolwork was often excruciating for my out-of-the-box, creative child, who wanted to do anything besides filling out a worksheet—especially a worksheet with numbers. But his is a story of miracles upon miracles, of God encouraging him with teachers who allowed him to go the extra mile and create a video instead of fill out a book report form, or discovering there was a computer-based math class that helped him overcome the fear of numbers and letters comingling together on a piece of paper.

Just a couple months ago, it was hard to hold back the tears of thanksgiving as he walked across the stage to receive his college diploma, wearing the gold cords around his neck, showing his hard-earned academic achievements. God truly answered our prayers and not only helped Elliott to persevere academically but to excel with high marks and great praise from his teachers and classmates.

Keep Praying!

Sometimes it's hard to pray for our kids' academics. We see them on their phones instead of studying, or we question the effort they put into their report or preparing for a test. They might pray for an A, but you think their effort was only worth a C. As we pray for our children's character, remember that we need to not only pray for our children's grades, but pray for their effort. Pray they will persevere and that they will learn good study habits, enjoy the subject, and absorb what's being taught. Pray especially for younger kids to have the opportunity to be taught in a way that fits their learning style.

....

We need to not only pray for our children's grades, but pray for their effort.

....

Pray They Are Filled with the Knowledge of God

I (Sally) often prayed for my children with this Scripture passage from Colossians 1:9-12:

> We continually ask God to fill you with the knowledge of his [God's] will through all the wisdom and understanding that the Spirit gives, so that you may live a life worthy of the Lord and please him in every way: bearing fruit in every good work, growing in the knowledge of God, being strengthened with all power according to his glorious might so that you may have great endurance and patience, and giving joyful thanks to the Father.

Our children need endurance and patience to persevere in academics. And their good work in school is to do their very best academically. In the book of Daniel, he and his three friends were to learn the Babylonian studies. They were the top students, never defiling themselves as they held on to God and His truths, soaring academically.

> To these four young men God gave knowledge and understanding of all kinds of literature and learning...At the end of the time set by the king to bring them into his service, the chief official presented them to Nebuchadnezzar. The king talked with them, and he found none equal to Daniel, Hananiah, Mishael and Azariah; so they entered the king's service. In every matter of wisdom and understanding about which the king questioned them, he found them ten times better than all the magicians and enchanters in his whole kingdom (Daniel 1:17-20).

Our children can do the same. All four of my children did well in school as I and other mothers prayed and encouraged them forward. Each of my four children had different abilities, learning styles, teachers, and struggles than the others. What was the same? I and others were praying God's Word over them each week. Persevering in prayer so they could persevere in school!

When my oldest began to have seizures in high school, the medicines prescribed to prevent and minimize them made it difficult for him to study and stay awake in class. He went from all As to barely passing. I was one of those moms on graduation day, cheering the loudest as he crossed the bridge to receive his high school diploma! He went on to graduate from college with a major in philosophy. Just like Daniel, he soared in his courses and never let go of God, reaching many for Christ on his campuses. He is now becoming a teacher.

I truly believe prayer made all the difference in my children's academic lives. A child can do well at school and still walk closely with Christ. As we pray, they will indeed bear fruit in every good work.

Scripture Prayers for Your Child's Academics

Whatever _____ does, may he/she work at it with
all his/her heart, as working for the Lord, not for humans.

FROM COLOSSIANS 3:23

Give to _____ knowledge and understanding
of all kinds of literature and learning.

FROM DANIEL 1:17

Empower _____ to be strong and work.
For the Lord Almighty is with him/her.

FROM HAGGAI 2:4

I pray that _____ will continue to grow in wisdom
and stature and in favor with the Lord and with people.

FROM 1 SAMUEL 2:26 AND LUKE 2:52

Help _____ know that You, Lord, give wisdom;
from Your mouth come knowledge and understanding.
You hold success in store for the upright. You are a shield
to those whose walk is blameless, for You guard the course
of the just and protect the way of Your faithful ones.

FROM PROVERBS 2:6-8

Allow _____ to understand that no discipline
seems pleasant at the time, but painful. Later on,
however, it produces a harvest of righteousness and
peace for those who have been trained by it.

FROM HEBREWS 12:11

Guide _____ in Your truth and teach
him/her, for You are God his/her Savior. May
his/her hope be in You all day long.

FROM PSALM 25:5

May _____ not follow the crowd in doing wrong.

From Exodus 23:2

Remind _____ that all hard work pays off.
But if all he/she does is talk, he/she will be poor.

From Proverbs 14:23

I pray that _____ trusts he/she is Your
handiwork, created in Christ Jesus to do good works,
which You prepared in advance for him/her to do.

From Ephesians 2:10

❧

*We also glory in our sufferings, because we know that
suffering produces perseverance; perseverance, character;
and character, hope. And hope does not put us to shame,
because God's love has been poured out into our hearts
through the Holy Spirit, who has been given to us.*

Romans 5:3-5

6

Praying for Protection

But the Lord is faithful, and he will strengthen
you and protect you from the evil one.

2 THESSALONIANS 3:3

In the middle of the day, as our thoughts turn toward our kids, our prayers are often "arrow prayers" of protection from an array of threats: school shootings, bullying, abuse, and from Satan getting one "gleeful moment" of having our children in his clutches. What can we do to stand in the gap for them? We can pray!

Many times, I (Cyndie) have prayed with friends for God to provide a "hedge of protection" around our kids. While we don't always get to fully understand the impact of these prayers, there are times when God's care and answered prayer is very evident. My friend, Cathy Menconi, shared with me how her daughter was in Israel with her college group, and God amazingly protected her and the other students from being killed as they walked through a crosswalk at the same time a car ran a red light and was headed right for them. The car was intercepted by another vehicle, which was hit. That driver miraculously survived the severe accident. The college students were just inches from the collision. The next day, during the worship service, that intersection happened to be the photo used as the backdrop for the song lyrics. These words were displayed over the intersection photo: "Protector of my life, You did not forsake me. Hallelujah." What a powerful example of how God is our protector!

At another time, Cathy's daughter called home to ask for prayer as she was preparing to drive back to her dorm during a storm. She had been visiting three friends who were hospitalized after a car accident—an accident that God had prevented Cathy's daughter from being a part of! At the time of their phone call, Cathy had no idea why her intercessory prayers were significant and urgent. Unbeknownst to her and her daughter, the reason there were no cars on the road was that everyone else had heard the hurricane warning and had shuttered themselves indoors.

God protected Cathy's daughter, and He also protected both of their hearts and minds as He prevented them from hearing the news of the hurricane until she was safely back at the dorm. They later saw the dramatic reports highlighting the devastation nearby: roofs torn off homes, cars blown over and twisted around trees. God had answered their prayers for protection beyond what they could've known to ask for by keeping them both calm during the two-hour drive and through a devastating hurricane!

Praying That God Will Protect Our Schools

Students who make it safely to school are not always protected. Unfortunately, this is made clear with each passing year and reports of violence in schools and threats posed by outsiders as well. We need to rise up and pray that God will place a hedge of protection around every single one of our schools and universities. We have seen horrific tragedies on campuses, including the senseless mass shootings that terrify students and staff. Scripture prayer is the weapon we must use to protect the children and schools before a tragedy happens.

I (Sally) have been asked numerous times by school staff members if a Moms in Prayer group can be implemented in the schools where they work. They have felt and witnessed the power of prayer and know there is protection as we pray. One principal who was not

a Christian shared with me how our prayers were like an umbrella
for his school.

••••••••••••••••••••••••••••••••••••

*We need to rise up and pray that God will place a
hedge of protection around every
single one of our schools and universities.*

••••••••••••••••••••••••••••••••••••

One of the most heartbreaking moments we can experience is
when we realize we should have been praying and haven't been. I listened to a brave, precious leader weeping as we joined together to
pray after a shooting at her children's school. Her Moms in Prayer
group began the year praying but stopped after a few months. They
were busy moms, and everything seemed to be going well for their
children and the school. But, horrifyingly, the school became the
target of yet another school shooting that took the lives of innocent children. Jesus tells us to keep on praying and to never give up
(Luke 18:1). Usually we quit praying when we are discouraged, but
sometimes we stop praying because everything seems to be going
well. Our children and schools always need our prayers! There is an
incredible battle for their souls! "The thief comes only to steal and
kill and destroy; I came that they may have life, and have it abundantly" (John 10:10 NASB).

Lord, embolden _____ against the thief who
comes only to steal and kill and destroy. Empower
him/her to have life and have it abundantly.

FROM JOHN 10:10 NASB

When we stand in the gap through prayer for schoolchildren and
staff, we defeat the enemy each time. Our students need protection

from drugs, alcohol, sexual addictions, false teachings, wrong choices, bad friends, suicide, and all kinds of harm the enemy desires to do to them. Luke 22:31-32 (NASB) says, "Simon, Simon, behold, Satan has demanded permission to sift you like wheat; but I have prayed for you, that your faith may not fail; and you, when once you have turned again, strengthen your brothers."

Every week, women meet to pray protection over their children and grandchildren and the schools the children attend. We pray that those who plan to do harm will be caught or have their plans deterred. God answers prayer. Just this year at our local community college, a student's plan to shoot fellow students was halted. I hear stories just like this one and other stories of drug dealers, sex offenders, and others being caught before harm comes to a campus.

Praying After a Tragedy

Sometimes we pray and tragedy still happens; yet, we see God moving and people coming to Christ in the middle of loss or troubles. The group of women who had stopped praying and then experienced tragedy in their school shed a lot of tears, but then they committed to the work of prayer. Now they are witnessing God's grace, mercy, and salvation happening in their community. Here is how a Moms in Prayer state coordinator describes what happened:

Unfortunately, too many schools have been riddled with gun-related tragedies this year. It weighs heavily on our heart when we see this kind of violence. As we prayed for the students, faculty, and families on a statewide prayer call, I know God brought hope and comfort in Jesus Christ in the darkest hours. At the time of this tragedy, Moms in Prayer International rallied to pray. We trusted that God "heals the brokenhearted and binds up their wounds" (Psalm 147:3).

Lord, heal up _____'s broken heart
and bind up his/her wounds.

FROM PSALM 147:3

What I witnessed in this tragedy was an all-powerful Creator gathering His people: Fellow churches in the community acted quickly to host a vigil on the day of the shooting. Several churches in the area were involved in the initial wave of outreach to the victims of the shooting, particularly those with students in their congregations who attend the school. He provided the only hope for the families (Psalm 3:2-6). He's the only One who can bring peace where there is nothing but loss and struggle and anger and fury and confusion (Psalm 29:11). He provided indicators to point to Himself, for us all to see Christ in the forefront of this tragedy (1 Peter 1:3-6).

My belief is that our heavenly Father does not leave His children in the depths of sorrow. Joy comes eventually, and it comes in God's timing. For me as the Moms in Prayer state coordinator, I saw a busy, relaxed MIP group leader convicted and set on fire by the circumstances this tragedy caused. I once had a group that seldom met; I now have one group that has divided into two, with prayers covering the school twice a week: one in the daytime, and one at night to accommodate working moms.

There are nutrients that we draw out of seasons of suffering which we can't get any other way. They strengthen the bones of our faith and sweeten the marrow. I know for certain our Lord is near to the brokenhearted and saves the crushed in spirit. There is a unique and special promised nearness that we will enjoy one day as we look to Him, our Savior, our strength.

Praying Against Fear

Linda Vogel of Texas shares this story of God's protection.

Hurricane Harvey settled overhead, dropping 50 inches of rain in August 2017. Our high school and many, many homes in our community were flooded. Our students had to begin the school year being bused to a distant high school. Many lost not only their high school, but their homes. In March 2018, students finally returned to their home high school. But many students are still not back in their family homes.

I observed a growing fear in the hearts of our community high school moms. They voiced fear of a school shooting. Kingwood parents needed reassurance for such a time as this. So I called up my old '80s high school prayer group (called Moms in Touch back then). And I contacted the current MIP high school group. We joined forces and created a plan to pray together. School permission was granted to do a Sunday prayer walk on the grounds of Kingwood High School. We stationed ourselves outside on the school grounds. We praised, gave thanks, and asked the Lord to establish His protective shield. Three generations participated: the original MITI moms, the current MIPI moms, and some of their children/grandchildren. Generational blessings flowed!

We are not victims. Prayer is the best response to a threat that we cannot humanly combat. We can comfort our stressed community moms with these reassuring words from Lamentations 2:19: We poured out our hearts before the Lord and lifted our hands...for the lives of our children.

> Arise, cry out in the night, as the watches of the night begin; pour out your heart like water in the presence of the Lord. Lift up your hands to him for the lives of your children, who faint from hunger at every street corner.
>
> Lamentations 2:19

Often, parental fear is what draws us to pray. Janet shares:

Our daughter had applied to law schools and was blown away and excited to be accepted to Harvard Law School. Although I knew it was a big honor and I was so proud of her, I was completely overwhelmed with a sense of fear. Fear that the environment would be anti-God, fear that they would mess with her mind with philosophies of life that seem so wise but are, in reality, foolish. God spoke to me through His Word: "It is the Lord who goes before you. He will be with you; he will not leave you or forsake you. Do not fear or be dismayed" (Deuteronomy 31:8 esv).

God was going before her. He would be and will always be with her and not forsake her. Why do I fear man when God's promises are so clear? God also showed me His sovereignty by her receiving emails from not one, but two Christian clubs from the law school. They were reaching out to her before she even began. He has His people everywhere. He also appointed a new dean of the law school who is more aligned with our beliefs. That was a miracle. My prayers for protection continue as she finishes up her first year, but with increased confidence and with a sound mind! God loves our daughter so much. He has her in the palm of His hand. Thank you, Lord!

Scripture Prayers for Protection

These can be prayed for a child or for a school or university. Along with the *he* and *she* pronouns, we also added *it* and *they* as an option when praying for academic institutions and staff.

> Do not grant the wicked their desires, Lord;
> do not let their plans succeed.
>
> Psalm 140:8

> May _____ be enthroned in Your presence forever;
> appoint Your love and faithfulness to protect him/her/it.
>
> From Psalm 61:7

> Lord, I know You are faithful. Strengthen _____
> and protect him/her/it from the evil one.
>
> From 2 Thessalonians 3:3

> Empower _____ to be alert and of sober mind,
> because his/her/its enemy the devil prowls around
> like a roaring lion looking for someone to devour.
>
> From 1 Peter 5:8

> Let all who take refuge in You be glad; let them ever
> sing for joy. Spread Your protection over _____,
> that those who love Your name may rejoice in You.
>
> From Psalm 5:11

> Father, may no one take _____ captive
> through hollow and deceptive philosophy, which
> depends on human tradition and the basic
> principles of this world rather than on Christ.
>
> From Colossians 2:8

Lord, keep _____ safe and protect
him/her/it forever from the wicked.

FROM PSALM 12:7

May integrity and uprightness protect _____,
because his/her/its hope, Lord, is in You.

FROM PSALM 25:21

Lord, be near to the brokenhearted at _____
school/university and save those who are crushed in spirit.

FROM PSALM 34:18 NASB

Lord, be _____'s hiding place; protect him/her/
it from trouble and surround him/her/it with songs of
deliverance. Instruct _____ and teach him/her/
[the staff] in the way he/she/they should go. Counsel
him/her/them with Your loving eye on him/her/them.

FROM PSALM 32:7-8

Lord, You command us to be strong and courageous.
Help _____ not be afraid or discouraged. Be
with _____ wherever he/she/they goes/go.

FROM JOSHUA 1:9

Remind _____ that his/her/its help comes
from You, the Maker of heaven and earth. You
will not let _____'s foot slip. You watch
over him/her/it and do not slumber.

FROM PSALM 121:2-3

Rescue _____, Lord, from evildoers; protect
him/her/it from the violent, who devise evil plans in
their hearts and stir up war every day. They make their
tongues as sharp as a serpent's; the poison of vipers is
on their lips. Keep _____ safe, Lord, from the

hands of the wicked; protect him/her/them from the violent, who devise ways to trip his/her/their feet.

From Psalm 140:1-4

May _____ not be conformed to this world but be transformed by the renewing of his/her/their mind(s), so that _____ may prove what the will of God is, that which is good and acceptable and perfect.

From Romans 12:2 nasb

Lord, embolden _____ against the thief who comes only to steal and kill and destroy. Empower him/her/them to have life and have it abundantly.

From John 10:10 nasb

◦⌒◦

I love you, Lord;
  you are my strength.
The Lord is my rock, my fortress, and my savior;
  my God is my rock, in whom I find protection.
He is my shield, the power that saves me,
  and my place of safety.
I called on the Lord, who is worthy of praise,
  and he saved me from my enemies.
The ropes of death entangled me;
  floods of destruction swept over me.
The grave wrapped its ropes around me;
  death laid a trap in my path.
But in my distress I cried out to the Lord;
  yes, I prayed to my God for help.
He heard me from his sanctuary;
  my cry to him reached his ears...

He reached down from heaven and rescued me;
  he drew me out of deep waters.
He rescued me from my powerful enemies,
  from those who hated me and were too
  strong for me.
They attacked me at a moment when I was in distress,
  but the LORD supported me.
He led me to a place of safety;
  he rescued me because he delights in me...

God's way is perfect.
  All the LORD's promises prove true.
  He is a shield for all who look to him
  for protection.
For who is God except the LORD?
  Who but our God is a solid rock?
God arms me with strength,
  and he makes my way perfect.
He makes me as surefooted as a deer,
  enabling me to stand on mountain heights.
He trains my hands for battle;
  he strengthens my arm to draw a bronze bow.
You have given me your shield of victory.
  Your right hand supports me;
  your help has made me great.
You have made a wide path for my feet
  to keep them from slipping.
I chased my enemies and caught them;
  I did not stop until they were conquered.

PSALM 18:1-6,16-19,30-37 NLT

7

Praying Through Suffering

And He has said to me, "My grace is sufficient for you, for power is
perfected in weakness." Most gladly, therefore, I will rather boast
about my weaknesses, so that the power of Christ may dwell in me.

2 Corinthians 12:9 NASB

As we pray God's Word over our children, we watch the story unfold from suffering to triumph in Christ. Both of my (Sally's) boys, who are young married men, have lifelong, life-altering, life-threatening diseases. And yet in their suffering is God's story to the world of abundant grace through Jesus Christ their Lord and Savior.

Some of the scriptures I pray frequently for my boys are familiar to most believers: Matthew 6:19-21 and 33-34:

> Do not store up for yourselves treasures on earth, where moth and rust destroy, and where thieves break in and steal. But store up for yourselves treasures in heaven, where neither moth nor rust destroys, and where thieves do not break in or steal; for where your treasure is, there your heart will be also...But seek first His kingdom and His righteousness, and all these things will be added to you. So do not worry about tomorrow; for tomorrow will care for itself. Each day has enough trouble of its own (NASB).

My son David had graduated college with a dual major, and if they would have allowed, he would have graduated with three degrees: finance, accounting, and management. After graduation, he was preparing for his CPA and an intense interview with a top accounting firm. He had his life planned out. Suddenly, without warning, his intestines ruptured and, after 12 days in the hospital, he was blessed to be alive.

> Lord, help _____ not store up for himself/herself treasures on earth, where moth and rust destroy and where thieves break in and steal. Empower him/her to seek first Your kingdom and righteousness, so all these things will be added to him/her. Help _____ not worry about tomorrow; for tomorrow will care for itself.
>
> From Matthew 6:19-21,33-34

After two days back home, he shared with me his heart. He said, "I asked God if I had only a few years to live, how would God want me to live." Because of that question and God's leading, David made a huge career change and now works in the medical industry. He serves God powerfully both in work and in life, impacting our area for Christ. Through suffering, God realigned his view to seek first God's kingdom and righteousness. While I would have loved God to have scooped down and prevented this illness, God used it to strengthen his faith and direction.

....

As we pray Scripture over our children, we watch the story unfold from suffering to triumph in Christ.

....

Suffering Can Strengthen Our Faith

Amanda Cant shares a similar story of how suffering strengthens our faith—and especially the faith of our children.

I grew up in a family that didn't go to church or talk with me about God. It's not that they didn't believe in Him, but going to church was not a priority. As a teenager, I was asked to attend church with a friend. We would have a sleepover on a Saturday and then go to church on Sunday with her family. I loved the message, family time, the Sunday school fun—and of course the donut at the end! After starting college, I took the step to commit my life to Jesus and was baptized. I loved how I was the one who committed my life to Christ. I was never forced, but always encouraged, and ultimately that was my plan for my children.

The day I became a mother was one of the best days of my life. Through all the excitement, pain, and sleepless nights, I saw first-hand God's beautiful work as I looked into my daughter's eyes. From her first breath to the present, I have prayed daily for her. I pray she follows God's Word and the journey He has for her. I pray that through her weakness, she will find strength in Him. I have prayed that one day she too would be baptized. However, I have not pressured my sweet Mackenzie into finding His love before she is ready to embrace it.

At three years old, I knew Mackenzie was going to change the world. She was maternal and strong. She was blessed with twin baby sisters, only to discover that one would not make it and the other would be fighting for her life. Additionally, both her grandfathers were diagnosed with cancer within months of each other. As I started to lose hope, God led me to 1 Corinthians 10:13, "No temptation has overtaken you except what is common to mankind. And God is faithful; he will not let you be tempted beyond what you can bear. But when you are tempted, he will also provide a way out so that you can endure it."

No temptation has overtaken _____ except what is common to mankind. You are faithful; please do not

let _____ be tempted beyond what he/she can
bear. Help her find the way out You've provided for her.

FROM 1 CORINTHIANS 10:13

He gave me strength to fight, and in turn I saw Mackenzie fight alongside me. Very few little girls know how to comfort their dying grandfather, have patience with a sister with special needs, and go to bed every night praying and thanking God for what she has, not for what she hopes she can have. I feared she might pull away from God, but I found her praying more through all these tragedies.

When Mackenzie was six, we packed up and moved from California to Colorado. We found an amazing church that welcomed us right away. Mackenzie started asking all kinds of questions about God. Baptism came up, and I explained to her what being baptized meant. After my explanation, she said, "Mom! Why have you not baptized me yet?" Talk about a mom fail! She seemed so young that it never crossed my mind. After she spoke with our pastor and children's ministry leader, they said she was ready. Before we knew it, Mackenzie was baptized, and when I saw her smile, I knew this had an incredible impact on her.

Today Mackenzie is seven. She has lost both grandfathers to cancer, lost a baby sister, and has watched her other sister fight and conquer all odds (now known as the miracle baby). Mackenzie speaks to friends about God and has such a huge heart for her community. In order to earn money for the foster children in our area, she drew pictures others could order, put together a hot cocoa stand, did chores around the house, and asked friends to help out as well. Through her efforts and others, our church raised $8,000 for foster kids.

Before bed one night, Mackenzie asked me how we know God is listening to our prayers. Before I could answer she said, "I know! God is doing things, and He is always listening."

The Beauty of God's Grace

We have one more story to share with you—especially those of you who are personally going through a time of suffering. Deena Kvasnik's story reveals the beauty of God's grace upon this young woman's life as her mother-in-law and her friends prayed for Deena.

As a mother I pray for my kids every day. It is a great gift and a privilege. Until recently, I underestimated how much I needed a praying mom in my own life. It was the prayers of my mother-in-law, a 20-plus-year veteran of Moms in Prayer, who impacted my desperate need for healing.

When I was two years old, my parents divorced, and from that moment on my life was a roller coaster of trauma, loneliness, fear, and anxiety. As a child, unconditional love and a sense of belonging were nonexistent. I learned to look to the attention of others for my self-worth and constantly worried about what others thought of me. Because of insecurity in my own home, I felt the need to earn love and adoration. Ashamed by this and severely self-conscious while growing up, I spent most of my youth trying to hide in the shadows. In high school I often ate my lunch alone in the girls' bathroom. I didn't have any knowledge of God or understanding of my identity in Christ and had no one praying for me or emotionally supporting me.

Without a praying mom in my life, my emotions started to control me in different ways. Fear of life, work, social rejection, and not being liked or admired eventually caused a continual gnawing, tight knot in my stomach. I quieted the fear by starving it and myself. This was comforting and made me feel safe, secure, and in control. However, at the same time I was numbing the pain, I was starving my body, killing it one day at a time.

Blindsided by how quickly anorexia had taken over, I was terribly ashamed. As a grown woman and someone who called herself a Christian, I felt like an imposter. I hid my eating disorder for years, becoming very thin and ill. The shame continued to grow to the point where I went into isolation, believing the lie that I was an unworthy wife and mother. I felt undeserving of God's love. My husband was very concerned and asked me to talk to someone.

Without a close relationship with my own mom, I went to my mother-in-law to tell her about the struggle with anorexia. As I explained the deep pit I was in, her response was, "Deena, I don't understand what you are going through since I have never experienced it, but what I can do is pray for you. Can I bring this to my Moms in Prayer group?" Desperate for help, I ignored the shame, embarrassment, and isolation that had controlled me for years and accepted her offer.

Knowing there was a group of women committed to praying for me weekly helped me come out of isolation and to realize it was okay to let others in and to be "found out." I started to share with some friends and to reengage in my community. I felt free, alive, and most importantly, I felt known by God.

I realized that to be known exactly where I was at, in the muck and mud of my sin, was okay because God loved me no matter what. I didn't have to be ashamed. I didn't have to hide. I didn't have to pretend.

In fact, I started to celebrate my imperfections! The more imperfect I admitted I was, the closer I grew to God. This was the best gift I've ever been given. And it is summed up in three words God gave me one day—with a very large period at the end.

I AM ENOUGH.

The period after the word *enough* is very important. For as long as I can remember, something that set a requirement, a condition always came before that period. "I am enough...*if* I have cool clothes. I am enough...because I nailed a great job. I am enough...because I am an amazing stay-at-home mom doing fantastic projects with my kids all day. I am enough...because I cook great meals for my family. I am enough...because I am skinny. I am enough...because people like me. And the list went on and on. The freedom that came from the realization that I am enough *period* was a turning point and allowed me to accept God's grace and His healing. It also opened the door to forgive myself, stripping away the guilt and shame that had isolated me. I finally believed I was worthy of God, motherhood, friendship, community, and love. That no matter what bad choices I made, nothing could make me undeserving of God's great love for me.

I believe with all my heart that this deep understanding of God's perfect love came to me through hours of prayer specifically by my mother-in-law, Elaine. The prayers of Elaine and her Moms in Prayer group changed the course of my life. She has met weekly with her group since the 1990s to pray for the school and students, and she'll say this is the highlight of her week. Elaine's example inspired me to join a group, and now more than 20 years later it has become the highlight of my week as well. I've learned that a praying mother is a great blessing to her family. A family without prayer is like a tree without roots (from Mark 4:17).

God has redeemed me through a praying mom! When I struggle (and I still do), it is a great blessing to know that my mother-in-law will pray for me. This experience has taught me many things. I am no longer ashamed of my imperfections or struggle with sin. God chose me to be the mother of my two children, and I don't have to be perfect in order to be worthy of that title. And everyone, even moms, need prayer...and those prayers matter! In Luke 18:1, Jesus tells us to, "Always pray and not give up."

Lord, help _____ always pray and not give up.

For those who are hurting or struggling, here are several life-giving revelations I discovered during my journey. I pray they encourage and help you:

Lean into the discomfort.

You are worthy of love and belonging.

Believe that what makes you vulnerable makes you beautiful.

When you try to numb one thing, you actually numb every-thing—your whole life.

If you are fighting with vulnerability, lose the fight, and you will gain your life back.

Allow yourself to be deeply seen.

Know whose you are: You are God's perfect creation, and He doesn't make mistakes.

Practice gratitude and lean into joy.

God loves you, always, every day, every night, no matter what.

You are enough.

Persevering During Difficulties

Rarely is there a life not marked by suffering. While we want to protect our kids from pain, often that's the very vessel God wants to use to bring our kids close to Him and to grow them more and more into His image.

In 2 Corinthians 1:8-11, Paul gives an example of the importance of intercessory prayer during times of suffering:

> We do not want you to be uninformed, brothers and sisters, about the troubles we experienced in the province of Asia. We were under great pressure, far beyond our ability to endure, so that we despaired of life itself. Indeed, we felt we had received the sentence of death. But this happened that

we might not rely on ourselves but on God, who raises the dead. He has delivered us from such a deadly peril, and he will deliver us again. On him we have set our hope that he will continue to deliver us, as you help us by your prayers. Then many will give thanks on our behalf for the gracious favor granted us in answer to the prayers of many.

Instead of praying only that God removes your child's suffering, pray they can persevere through a trial, and God will use it to create growth in their life. Pray they don't get entangled by sin and will instead fix their eyes on Jesus during the trial. That way they won't grow weary and lose heart, they will depend on God, and they will set their hope on Christ.

Scripture Prayers for Endurance

Remind _____ to call on You in the day of
trouble; deliver him/her, so he/she will honor You.

FROM PSALM 50:15

Lord, encourage _____ to rejoice when he/
she runs into problems and trials, for we know they
help us develop endurance. And endurance develops
strength of character, and character strengthens our
confident hope of salvation. And this hope will not
lead to disappointment. Help _____ know
how dearly You love us, because You have given us
the Holy Spirit to fill our hearts with Your love.

FROM ROMANS 5:3-5 NLT

Lord, help _____ consider it pure joy
whenever he/she faces trials of many kinds, because
he/she knows that the testing of his/her faith
produces perseverance. Encourage him/her to let
perseverance finish its work so that he/she may be
mature and complete, not lacking anything.

FROM JAMES 1:2-4

For the glory of Your name, O Lord, preserve
_____'s life. Because of Your faithfulness,
bring _____ out of this distress.

FROM PSALM 143:11 NLT

Lord, help _____ always pray and not give up.

FROM LUKE 18:1

Lord, Your grace is sufficient for _____, for Your
power is made perfect in weakness. Help him/her boast
all the more gladly about his/her weaknesses, so that

Your power may rest on him/her. May _____
delight in weaknesses, in insults, in hardships, in
persecutions, in difficulties, for Your sake. For when
he/she is weak, then he/she will be strong in You.

From 2 Corinthians 12:9-12

No temptation has overtaken _____ except
what is common to mankind. You are faithful,
please do not let _____ be tempted
beyond what he/she can bear. Help him/her find
the way out You've provided for him/her.

From 1 Corinthians 10:13

Lord, help _____ not store up for himself/herself
treasures on earth, where moth and rust destroy and
where thieves break in and steal. Empower him/her to
seek first Your kingdom and righteousness, so all these
things will be added to him/her. Help _____ not
worry about tomorrow; for tomorrow will care for itself.

From Matthew 6:19,33-34 nasb

Therefore, since _____ is surrounded by such a
great cloud of witnesses, let him/her throw off everything
that hinders and the sin that so easily entangles. And let
_____ run with perseverance the race marked out
for him/her, fixing his/her eyes on Jesus, the pioneer and
perfecter of faith. For the joy set before You, Lord, You
endured the cross, scorning its shame, and sat down at the
right hand of the throne of God…Empower _____
not to grow weary and lose heart. Help him/her to endure
hardship as discipline, as You are treating him/her as Your
child…No discipline seems pleasant at the time, but
painful. Help _____ allow this difficulty to produce
a harvest of righteousness and peace in his/her life.

From Hebrews 12:1-3,7,11

❧

Hear me, LORD, and answer me,
    for I am poor and needy.
Guard my life, for I am faithful to you;
    save your servant who trusts in you.
You are my God;
have mercy on me, Lord,
    for I call to you all day long.
Bring joy to your servant, Lord,
    for I put my trust in you.
You, Lord, are forgiving and good,
    abounding in love to all who call to you.
Hear my prayer, LORD;
    listen to my cry for mercy.
When I am in distress, I call to you,
    because you answer me...

Teach me your way, LORD,
    that I may rely on your faithfulness;
give me an undivided heart,
    that I may fear your name.
I will praise you, Lord my God, with all my heart;
    I will glorify your name forever.
For great is your love toward me;
    you have delivered me from the depths,
    from the realm of the dead.
Arrogant foes are attacking me, O God;
    ruthless people are trying to kill me—
    they have no regard for you.
But you, Lord, are a compassionate and gracious God,
    slow to anger, abounding in love
    and faithfulness.
Turn to me and have mercy on me;

show your strength in behalf of your servant;
save me, because I serve you
just as my mother did.
Give me a sign of your goodness,
that my enemies may see it and be put to shame,
for you, LORD, have helped me and comforted me.

PSALM 86:1-7,11-17

8

Praying for Peace

Don't worry about anything; instead, pray about everything.
Tell God what you need, and thank him for all he has
done. Then you will experience God's peace, which exceeds
anything we can understand. His peace will guard
your hearts and minds as you live in Christ Jesus.

PHILIPPIANS 4:6-7 NLT

Sadly, many parents, schools, and communities are noticing an increase in the number of kids who are struggling with anxiety, depression, and suicidal thoughts. When we add to that the prevalence of addiction to drugs, alcohol, cutting, pornography, gaming, etc., none of us has to look beyond our neighborhoods to find students desperately in need of prayer. It can feel hopeless. Yet, in Philippians 4:6-7 God promises that if we hand Him our worries and anxieties, He will replace them with His peace. What an amazing spiritual exchange! Unfortunately, in the midst of the whirlwind of life, we can do the exact opposite: cling to our worries and let go of our sense of peace in the Lord. For our kids, the potential to spiral into fear and worry can be overwhelming. Often they're surrounded by digital peer pressure to act, do, say, and be a certain way. That is a recipe for anxiety. Yet God is faithful and promises to give us and our kids His peace.

Recently, I (Cyndie) was juggling several important work projects while also helping my college freshman daughter prepare for dorm life in another state, and encouraging my son in his postcollege "adulting" adventure. I was feeling overly stretched when a verse jumped out at me during my quiet time: "The LORD gives strength to his people; the LORD blesses his people with peace" (Psalm 29:11). Every time the overbearing to-dos started wrapping a not-so-subtle noose around my neck, I would repeat the verse. Sometimes I said it in my mind, and sometimes I spoke it aloud to others as we discussed tasks that needed to be done.

> Lord, give Your strength to _____;
> bless him/her with peace.
>
> FROM PSALM 29:11

No matter what is on your to-do list for today or tomorrow, no matter what large stress is looming in front of you, truly the peace of Christ can quiet the anxiety fogging up your mind. The result is beautifully explained in Isaiah 32:17, "The fruit of that righteousness will be peace; its effect will be quietness and confidence forever." Being right with God allows His peace to flourish in our lives, and from that peace blossoms a restorative combination of quietness and confidence.

....

God promises that if we hand Him our worries and anxieties, He will replace them with His peace.

....

As I share in *God-Confident Kids: Helping Your Child Find True Purpose, Passion and Peace,* when I was a teen, fear and anxiety filled my brain daily and diminished my God-given purpose. But meditating on Psalm 46 helped me release that fear and anxiety to God.

Psalm 46:1-7,10-11

God is our refuge and strength,
    an ever-present help in trouble.
Therefore we will not fear, though the earth give way
    and the mountains fall into the heart of the sea,
though its waters roar and foam
    and the mountains quake with their surging.
There is a river whose streams make glad the city of God,
    the holy place where the Most High dwells.
God is within her, she will not fall;
    God will help her at break of day.
Nations are in uproar, kingdoms fall;
    he lifts his voice, the earth melts.
The LORD Almighty is with us;
    the God of Jacob is our fortress...
He says, "Be still, and know that I am God;
    I will be exalted among the nations,
    I will be exalted in the earth."
The LORD Almighty is with us;
    the God of Jacob is our fortress.

When Professional Help Is Needed

Meditating on such powerful scriptures can help quiet the fear and anxiety that can take our brains hostage. Yet, sometimes it's important to seek the advice of a professional Christian counselor or medical doctor. Especially if your child seems depressed, has started isolating himself/herself, has stopped participating in activities, sleeps more or less, or eats more or less, it's wise to get professional help. And if you have any concern at all that your child might be considering suicide, be sure to seek professional help immediately. God often uses therapists to provide clarity when life seems overwhelming. Pray that God directs you to the best counselor for you or your child; pray for godly wisdom and insight for the counselor, and for open minds for you and/or your child to hear and accept what is being suggested. In the midst of the darkness, pray fervently that Satan will not get one gleeful moment.

Strength for a New School Year

Here is one of three stories from different perspectives about how God brought peace to anxious hearts. Lori Bittenbender, a mom of three in North Texas, shares this story:

> can do all things through Christ who strengthens me" (Philippians 4:13 NKJV) is a scripture I pray often for my kids. It's usually prayed with a tightness in my stomach and an "only God can help her now" sigh. I know many fellow moms have prayed this scripture over their kids for a variety of situations:
>
> - when their child has a long day ahead of them
> - when their child has a big test or a scary in-front-of-the-class presentation
> - when their child has to be brave and face something challenging: Hello driver's ed and cheer tryouts!
>
> It's normal for nerves and anxiety levels to run high on the first day of school. But for my daughter, who is extremely shy, first-day jitters tend to last a couple of months as she eases into the transition of a new school year, a new teacher, a new class, new classmates, and new routines.
>
> Lord, help _____ know he/she can do all
> things through Christ who strengthens him/her.
>
> FROM PHILIPPIANS 4:13
>
> I'm grateful for fellow Moms in Prayer warriors who have

prayed for strength for my daughter as she faces her anxieties and eases into feeling comfortable at school. So what strength did the Lord provide for my daughter, who is quite introverted?

- mouthing her reading words to her teacher until she was finally ready to read them out loud
- the ability to get through the day with a substitute teacher
- calmness with a walk around the block when a panic attack threatened to overtake her
- the desire to participate in show-and-tell

I didn't even know my daughter was going to have such high anxiety as she entered first grade. But God did. For two years now, He has provided us with understanding and compassionate teachers who did not judge my daughter but were patient with her and did all that they could to help her feel comfortable.

I always explain to my daughter's new teachers that she probably won't talk in class for the first six weeks. But I reassure them that she will be listening, observing, and learning. So, in order to communicate, her second-grade teacher gave my daughter a journal so she could write down what she wanted to say. I thank God for this brilliant idea. This precious journal is filled with the struggles my daughter's little body was facing due to nerves:

- My belly hurts.
- My wrist hurts.
- I miss my mom.

It's filled with fun things she wanted to share with her teacher:

- I get to go to the pool today.
- Look at my necklace!

It shares her fears:

- Is there going to be a sub tomorrow?
- Do you have lunch or recess duty? (My daughter felt more at ease if her teacher was in the cafeteria or on the playground with her class.)

Each week in Moms in Prayer we prayed for my daughter to have strength, to find her voice, and to feel comfortable. As those prayers were slowly answered, I would rejoice. I celebrated many moments.

- A teacher came up to me and said, "Your daughter talked to me today." I responded with a bit of shock, "She spoke to you?"
- She was able to use her voice to read a passage for an assessment.
- (One of my favorites) She was so comfortable with a substitute teacher, she asked if they could have lunch together!
- About three months into the school year, my daughter wrote on the final page of her journal:
- "I don't think I need my journal anymore!"

I am thankful that God knows my daughter's fears, knows where my daughter needs strength, and His grace brings her through each new school year.

Prayer Matters

Here's another testimony of God bringing peace to an anxious heart.

Sixteen years ago, I drove to an unfamiliar church and sat down among a dozen or so women. Looking back, I can say that was the start of a journey that has changed my life.

The first time I heard about Moms in Prayer, I was drawn to it, not because I was good at praying, but because I wasn't and wanted to be. Sitting in the midst of that gathering of women for one hour each week, I learned so much about prayer. There are many stories I could tell, but one story about my daughter, Melissa, is such a clear testimony of the impact of the time spent praying.

Melissa was a sophomore in high school and was having constant headaches, getting sick often, and having a tough time. We had seen the allergist, the ENT, the neurologist, leaving each with no clear answers. I remember going to my prayer hour week after week and crying, every time. I begged the Lord to make her well, to get us through this hard time, to give my husband, Ralph, and me wisdom as to what to do.

We had a prayer sheet for each week that detailed the scriptures we praised God with and the intercession verse selected for that week. I took notes on it about the answers to prayer we recognized and the specific requests we lifted up.

But in my notes, I can also look back and see that I prayed Psalm 50:15 for her: "May Melissa call upon You in the day of trouble. You will deliver Melissa, and she will glorify You." And Ephesians 3:20: "Do immeasurably more in Melissa's life than I could ask for or imagine, according to Your power that is at work in Melissa." Also Psalm 16:11: "Make known to Melissa the path of life."

Do immeasurably more than we ask or imagine, according
to Your power that is at work within _____.

FROM EPHESIANS 3:20

Week followed week. We prayed, and I cried. She was in bed for two weeks around Thanksgiving. After the holidays, she slowly got better, and I never really knew what happened. It wasn't until much later—and very recently—that I was privy to the rest of the story, which has become Melissa's testimony.

While I was praying that nothing Melissa went through would be wasted, she was struggling with not only physical issues, but a depression that led her to do something that could have taken her life. Instead, it brought about an awakening in her of how valuable her life truly is. Though she had already professed her faith in Christ, this was the time in her life that her faith became her own, and she gave her future completely over to Him.

Through her struggles, the Lord taught her how to walk with Him. During that time, He confirmed to her the calling to be a physician, so she could help others. Now as a third-year medical student, Melissa shared with me about a patient whose troubles seemed to have more of a psychological component than the patient wanted to admit. Melissa was able to share about her own struggle with depression and pray with this woman.

Looking back, my cup overflows with thankfulness to God for answering our prayers to carry her through and for indeed doing more than I could even fathom! I still struggle to carve out my morning prayer times for which I have daily lists—missionaries one day, our government another day, in addition to others. But I continue to do it, though imperfectly, because I believe God has called me to be an intercessor. And the greatest fuel to that fire is my weekly prayer with my Moms in Prayer buddies. I heard this in Moms in Prayer: "Like redwood trees in a forest, we stand connected as a network of strength, beholding new dimensions of God's power. We are pulling our children to safety like troops invading enemy territory."

Prayer matters.

Though prayer is extremely important for every aspect of our lives, MIP focuses on prayer for our children and schools. As one grandmother who prayed with us said, "Just as God has equipped us to labor to bring our babies into the world, so He has called us to travail in prayer for each one." Moms in Prayer has discipled me in prayer. I loved hearing those women praise and thank Him, and the most amazing part was to hear how the Holy Spirit would lead another mom to pray for my child. She could not have known what we were going through, but so often another mom brought out aspects of the situation I had not thought of that were right on target.

Sharing struggles through prayer, with confidentiality, creates an indescribable bond. These women have wrestled in prayer with me through tough teachers, middle school drama, boyfriends and girlfriends, sicknesses, college and career choices, the birth of grandbabies, and so much more. God has been so faithful. His faithfulness is often highlighted through the support of God-fearing women who are sometimes quicker than I to recognize God's hand and His answer to prayers we have prayed.

Living Out Philippians 4

Have you personally experienced giving your worries to God and allowing Him to fill you with His inexplicable peace? Or maybe you were in the midst of stress, but you suddenly felt an overwhelming peace and found out later someone was praying for you. When God's peace descends upon us in times of chaos, that change is remarkable.

We write more about this specifically in *Unshaken* and the *Unshaken Study Guide*. Praying through the four steps of prayer—praise, confession, thanksgiving, and intercession—helps us move from fear to prayer. The situation might remain the same, but God promises to fill us with His peace when we hand Him our fears, anxieties, and worries.

We connected with Libby McCandless as a result of our book *Unshaken*. She shares:

I have a date marked next to Philippians 4:6-7—April 4, 2017—and every time I think of that time or read that passage again, my eyes fill with tears as I recall how God gave me this verse to pray so that He could be glorified. I had just been reading the chapter in *Unshaken* on praise and the amazing illustration of 2 Chronicles 20 for "Fighting the Enemy with Praise." I gained a newfound understanding on how praising God should precede any battle we are about to fight...and we had one on the horizon. After several months of conversations with a new potential employer, Todd was being flown out to California for the final round of interviews. Everything hinged on this trip and the impression he would make. He left St. Louis on a Monday evening with interviews starting early the next morning, and after eight months of rejections, discouragement, and financial strain, he had some big enemies to face: self-doubt, fear, the enemy's lies that he wasn't good enough for the job.

That night, as I wrote in my prayer journal and reread my now dog-eared copy of *Unshaken*, this verse jumped out at me, and I knew the Lord was giving it to me to pray for my husband: "You will not have to fight this battle. Take up your positions; stand firm and see the deliverance the LORD will give you, Judah and Jerusalem. Do not be afraid; do not be discouraged. Go out to face them tomorrow, and the LORD will be with you" (2 Chronicles 20:17). I texted the verse to my husband and told him that I was praying this verse on his behalf, that I knew tomorrow he would "go out to face them" and that the Lord would be with him. I was filled with a peace and assurance I have rarely experienced before. I knew the Lord would fight the battle for him: "For the battle is not yours, but God's" (2 Chronicles 20:15).

Todd received and accepted the job offer and is now celebrating almost a year working there. And an amazing postscript: At the beginning of this year, the company made some upper-level decisions (for reasons that had nothing to do with Todd), eliminating Todd's entire division, including his job. While normally our reaction would be complete panic, we had complete peace—knowing that God had brought him to this job for a reason, and He wouldn't abandon us. Well, thanks to many "divine appointments" with high-ranking employees, Todd had managed to impress many people in his short time at the new company, and they had no intentions of letting him leave—so they found him a new role within the company, with a bigger job description, better future, and a raise to boot.

It's easy to praise God on this side of our adventure, but I am convinced that when you make a sacrifice of praise (Hebrews 13:15) when things are at their worst, God is able to prove that He is in control and that He is good—*all* the time.

Scripture Prayers to Overcome Anxiety with the Peace of Christ

Empower _____ not to be anxious about anything, but in every situation, by prayer and petition, with thanksgiving, help _____ present his/her requests to You, Lord, and let the peace of God, which transcends all understanding, guard his/her heart and mind in Christ Jesus.

From Philippians 4:6-7

When anxiety is great within _____, may Your consolation bring him/her joy.

From Psalm 94:19

Lord, help _____ know and experience that You have not given us a spirit of fear, but of power and of love and of a sound mind.

From 2 Timothy 1:7 nkjv

Lord, help _____ experience the fruit of righteousness, which is peace, and the effect, which is quietness and confidence forever.

From Isaiah 32:17

For the glory of Your name, O Lord, preserve _____'s life. Because of Your faithfulness, bring _____ out of this distress.

From Psalm 143:11 nlt

Lord, help _____ know he/she can do all things through Christ who strengthens him/her.

From Philippians 4:13

Help _____ not fear, for You are with him/

her; help him/her not be dismayed, for You are his/
her God. Strengthen _____ and help him/
her. Uphold him/her by Your righteous right hand.

FROM ISAIAH 41:10

Lord, please do immeasurably more than we
ask or imagine, according to Your power
that is at work within _____.

FROM EPHESIANS 3:20

Lord, help _____ experience the fruit of the
Spirit, which is love, joy, peace, forbearance, kindness,
goodness, faithfulness, gentleness, and self-control.

FROM GALATIANS 5:22-23

Lord give strength to _____ and
bless him/her with peace.

FROM PSALM 29:11

Help _____ cast all his/her anxiety on
You because You care for _____.

FROM 1 PETER 5:7

Let the peace of Christ rule in _____'s
heart, since as a member of one body he/she was
called to peace. And help him/her be thankful.

FROM COLOSSIANS 3:15

～

Do not fret because of those who are evil
or be envious of those who do wrong;
for like the grass they will soon wither,
like green plants they will soon die away.

Trust in the LORD and do good;
  dwell in the land and enjoy safe pasture.
Take delight in the LORD,
  and he will give you the desires of your heart.
Commit your way to the LORD;
  trust in him and he will do this:
He will make your righteous reward
  shine like the dawn,
  your vindication like the noonday sun.
Be still before the LORD
  and wait patiently for him;
do not fret when people succeed in their ways,
  when they carry out their wicked schemes.
Refrain from anger and turn from wrath;
  do not fret—it leads only to evil.
For those who are evil will be destroyed,
  but those who hope in the LORD will inherit the land.

PSALM 37

9

Praying for Freedom
from Addiction

*He reached down from on high and took hold of me; he drew me
out of deep waters. He rescued me from my powerful enemy, from
my foes, who were too strong for me. They confronted me in the day
of my disaster, but the LORD was my support. He brought me out
into a spacious place; he rescued me because he delighted in me.*

PSALM 18:16-19

L ast month as I (Sally) was walking into church, I saw the beautiful face of a young woman whom I had not seen in over a
decade. I ran to her, and we hugged unashamedly for a long time.
She knew I had been praying for her.

When she was two years old, she was in my Sunday school class.
She was so full of life and joy. Her dad is a pastor and missionary,
and her mom is a beautiful Christian woman. They passionately
love God, their family, and the church family. Yet, I witnessed this
girl grow into a teenager, and then too soon drugs stole her away
for over a decade. Oh, how the enemy loves to steal and rob. I kept
praying for her using the only weapon I know: God's Word. I often
prayed Luke 22:31-32 for her: "Simon, Simon, behold, Satan has
demanded permission to sift you like wheat; but I have prayed for
you, that your faith may not fail; and you, when once you have
turned again, strengthen your brothers" (NASB). By the power of
Christ, today this young woman is free of drugs and helping others

do the same. Her anger is gone, and she is again filled with life and joy. All thanks to God.

Witnessing this wholehearted transformation that only God could create reminded me of another family's story. Years ago, I was driving to a prayer event with a precious mom, who would soon become a dear friend. She showed me a picture of her son, who had many tattoos and piercings, and shared how she was part of a Moms in Prayer group who prayed fervently for their prodigals—those who have walked away from the Lord. Some of the moms in her group prayed their children would be caught by the police so they would not be killed by the drug dealers. I couldn't imagine what these moms were going through. But I watched this woman pray boldly for her son, never giving up. She would pray scripture prayers, like Jeremiah 24:7: "I will give them a heart to know Me, for I am the Lord; and they will be My people, and I will be their God, for they will return to Me with their whole heart" (NASB).

Soon she was sharing with me that her son had begun a Bible study in their home. She was cautious because it was an up-and-down journey for him. But Jeremiah 24:7 was answered powerfully in his life. He became a missionary in India as a young man. He served there for several years, marrying a pastor's daughter, having two daughters, and sharing Christ with many. He is now a pastor in the USA serving God with his whole heart. What will God do in your child's life as you boldly pray for them to return to Him with their whole hearts?

> Give _____ a heart to know You for You are the Lord, and we are Your people. Return _____ to You with his/her whole heart and be his/her God.
>
> From Jeremiah 24:7 NASB

Yearning for God in the Middle of Distress

Allow me to share one more story. What a privilege it is for us to bear witness to God's work in people's lives. When I first met Elise Attanasio, I saw a beautiful, gentle, soft-spoken woman of God. Then she shared her story of a hard, yet victorious battle for her son. I saw a mighty prayer warrior who understood how to use the weapon of praying God's Word. Her son, Devon, was addicted for over 15 years, and she was fighting for his life. For years, she poured out her heart in prayer using God's powerful Word. And God's Word brought hope and victory to her and her son. Here's her story about the power of Psalm 42:5: "Why are you cast down, O my soul? And why are you disquieted within me? Hope in God, for I shall yet praise Him for the help of His countenance" (NKJV).

More than ten years after the beginning of my son's battle with addiction, he entered several years of what I call a Life or Death Trap. This repetitive stanza from Psalm 42 and Psalm 43 was a place I could go to be real before the Lord. As a mom I was NOT OKAY. I needed the help of God's countenance to believe that "I shall yet praise Him." By the end of both psalms, the wording changes to "the help of my countenance and my God." And I found my joy again.

> Reach down from on high and take hold of
> _____; draw him/her out of deep waters. Rescue
> _____ from his/her powerful enemy, from
> his/her foes, who are too strong for him/her.
>
> FROM PSALM 18:16-17

My girlfriend called one day and told me I should begin a prodigal prayer group because everywhere she went her friends were talking about their wayward kids. After declining, I quickly realized this *was* for me! Four years later my group remains strong and committed. We pray for school-age and adult children and grandchildren to be delivered and set free to come back to faith in Christ. Three of my lovely ladies have become very capable leaders, and we still receive new moms from time to time.

I'm excited to share that Devon was set free from addictions. The addiction was too strong for him alone to defeat, but the moment he surrendered it to the Lord, he was set free. Devon calls his mom a prayer warrior who has her own "war room." She kept praying for him, never giving up. The power of prayer can bring your child home to the Lord!

A Prodigal's Perspective

We love hearing stories from prodigals. One young woman shared how she accepted Jesus into her heart at age ten, but that's not where her testimony ends.

When I was 17 years old, I got mixed up with the wrong crowd and started running from God. I was fascinated by the crowd's dark clothes, piercings, chains, spikes, and studs. I moved out of my loving parents' home and moved in with the guy I was dating at the time. He was very verbally and emotionally abusive to me. There were many more after him who became physically and sexually abusive as well.

At 18 years of age, I started smoking marijuana. I lived with several drug dealers, so my usage of the drug soon escalated to every day. I started burning Bibles and smoking marijuana out of the Bible paper. I wanted nothing to do with God. Somewhere around the age of 19, prescription pills crept into my life. A year later at the young age of 20, I started injecting methamphetamine into my veins daily. I saw many things humans were not intended to see and did things humans were not intended to do.

Following the extreme addiction of the needle, I soon lost everything I had to drugs. My car, my clothes, my friends, even my I.D. and birth certificate were taken from me by people I thought were my friends. I started selling drugs and living promiscuously with several meth dealers. Soon afterward, many of my dealers got busted. I was so tired of my life of drugs, sex, and crime, but I could not quit. I felt like there was no way out!

This dear one's story didn't end in defeat. After a fumbled attempt at suicide, she thought to herself, "I've tried everything else; maybe I can try God." She lay down, face to the ground, and really prayed for the first time in five years! The next morning she called her parents and asked them to come pick her up. God had prepared the last bed in the rehab center just for her, and she recovered there for two months.

She says, "Now I am home and am better than ever. I attend church, Narcotics Anonymous meetings, and Celebrate Recovery meetings. Now Jesus is real to me. So, moms everywhere, don't quit praying! My mom and her three other Moms in Prayer women are the 'angels' who prayed me out of hell."

....

Now Jesus is real to me. So, moms everywhere, don't quit praying!

....

Scripture Prayers for Freedom from Addiction

Rescue _____, O my God, out of
the hand of the wicked, out of the grasp
of the wrongdoer and ruthless man.

FROM PSALM 71:4 NASB

Turn Your ear to _____, come quickly
to his/her rescue; be _____'s rock of
refuge, a strong fortress to save him/her.

FROM PSALM 31:2

Rescue the weak and the needy; deliver
_____ from the hand of the wicked.

FROM PSALM 82:4

Give _____ a new heart and put a new spirit
in him/her. Take out his/her stony, stubborn heart
and give _____ a tender, responsive heart.

FROM EZEKIEL 36:26 NLT

Lord, keep _____ from deliberate sins!
Don't let them control him/her. Empower him/
her to be free of guilt and innocent of great sin.

FROM PSALM 19:13 NLT

In the distant future, when _____ is suffering
all these things, bring him/her to finally return to
You, Lord, and to listen to what You tell him/her.

FROM DEUTERONOMY 4:30 NLT

For the waywardness of the simple will kill them,
and the complacency of fools will destroy them;

but help _____ listen to You and live in
safety and be at ease, without fear of harm.

FROM PROVERBS 1:32-33

Deliver _____ from evildoers and save him/
her from those who are after his/her blood.

FROM PSALM 59:2

Reach down from on high and take hold of
_____; draw him/her out of deep waters.
Rescue _____ from his/her powerful enemy,
from his/her foes, who are too strong for him/her.

FROM PSALM 18:16-17

Bring _____ out into a spacious place;
rescue him/her because You delight in him/her.

FROM PSALM 18:19

Help _____ walk before You faithfully and with
wholehearted devotion and do what is good in Your eyes.

FROM 2 KINGS 20:3

Give _____ a heart to know You, for You are the
Lord, and we are Your people. Return _____ to
You with his/her whole heart and be his/her God.

FROM JEREMIAH 24:7 NASB

∽

I waited patiently for the LORD;
*   he turned to me and heard my cry.*
He lifted me out of the slimy pit,
*   out of the mud and mire;*
he set my feet on a rock

and gave me a firm place to stand.
He put a new song in my mouth,
    a hymn of praise to our God.
Many will see and fear the LORD
    and put their trust in him.

PSALM 40:1-3

10

Praying for Relationships

As iron sharpens iron, so a friend sharpens a friend.

PROVERBS 27:17 NLT

The relationships our kids have at school can either be the high-light of their day or spur deep heartache. God uses other people throughout our lives to be irons who sharpen iron, to help shape us into who God wants us to be. So while we want to pray that our children will have only amazing friendships, God might be using the more difficult relationships to fulfill 2 Corinthians 4:17: "For momentary, light affliction is producing for us an eternal weight of glory far beyond all comparison" (NASB).

> As iron sharpens iron, Lord help _____
> and _____ sharpen each other in a positive
> way, to help them grow in Christlike character.
>
> FROM PROVERBS 27:17

For those of us with more than one child, we never like to see our children fight. It breaks our hearts. If they disagree and learn to understand their differences, that is good. But if the tensions and the comments become hurtful, and the siblings don't want to spend time together as they grow, that creates a house divided. Our children, at every age, must learn to be patient with one another and love one another unconditionally.

As a young mom, I (Sally) regularly listened to Dr. James Dobson on the radio. He would share how our homes should be a safe place for our growing children. I desired my children to be kind to each other and to become lifelong friends. They are grown now with lives of their own, and God answered my prayers richly. They are all different, with different careers and different friends, yet they love each other, and they love to spend time together. It amazes me when they or their spouses send out a text saying it's time to hang out again, and it has only been a few weeks or days since the last time.

I would often pray through Ephesians for my children, and when I see them together now, it is Ephesians 4:1-3 that is so evident. And Ephesians 4:29-32 are the verses I am grateful to have prayed and continue to pray for the family.

Ephesians 4:1-3

> I urge you to live a life worthy of the calling you have received. Be completely humble and gentle; be patient, bearing with one another in love. Make every effort to keep the unity of the Spirit through the bond of peace.

Ephesians 4:29-32

> Do not let any unwholesome talk come out of your mouths, but only what is helpful for building others up according to their needs, that it may benefit those who listen. And do not grieve the Holy Spirit of God, with whom you were sealed for the day of redemption. Get rid of all bitterness, rage and anger, brawling and slander, along with every form of malice. Be kind and compassionate to one another, forgiving each other, just as in Christ God forgave you.

Lord, help _____ experience how
wonderful and pleasant it is when brothers
and sisters live together in harmony!

FROM PSALM 133:1 NLT

I prayed they would each have best friends who love Christ. Many of their best friends have been a part of their lives since elementary school and were the kids of other Moms in Prayer women. Today these relationships continue to bless my children with encouragement, edification, and accountability toward Christ. As Proverbs 17:17 says, "A friend loves at all times."

Praying for College Roommates

As your children head into adulthood, keep praying for their friends and relationships. And don't forget to pray for their roommates, especially for college roommates. Nothing tries one's patience and conflict resolution skills more than being crammed into a tiny dorm room with one—or more!—other strangers. I (Cyndie) knew I would be praying hard for this area of my son Elliott's life. By the time he registered in the spring of his senior year in high school, many of the dorms had been filled. So as a freshman, he was bound for a triple dorm that shared living space with another set of three guys. Thankfully, the school allowed students to look at profile summaries of potential roommates. Most of the guys expressed passion for gaming or sports—neither of which were of interest to Elliott.

We continued praying, and we discovered a dorm with two musicians from Christian homes. What he found out later was that his three other suite mates, with whom he shared a living space, were also musicians. The guys would occasionally jam together and enjoyed their shared interest. Conflicts were at a minimum, and Elliott ended up rooming with one of the guys for three years, until his senior year, when he roomed with three other film majors.

I recently helped my daughter, Zoe, pack and head off to her freshman year of college. She wanted to go to the same university as her brother and had been working toward that goal for a year. Knowing that she is an introvert and that she's used to having personal space to regroup, I started praying early on for her future roommates. God was so gracious in His provision. In her senior English class, she and her friend from dance sat at the same table with two other young Christian women—all who decided to go to the same college. Zoe, her friend, and her friend's twin decided to room together, and that has been such a blessing. This gives my introvert daughter the chance to feel like she comes home to "family" every day. The added blessing is that one of her friends is outgoing and will no doubt encourage both her sister and Zoe to participate in various activities. And the twin sister is an introvert who will understand and respect the importance of having personal space and quiet. They all can sit quietly and happily on their beds, recharging their personal batteries before going back into a sea of people. This blessing from God has made the transition from home to "adulting" a little easier.

When School Relationships Are Difficult

Most of us and our kids have had to deal with difficult relationships at school, and God uses these as "iron sharpens iron." Louisa Chiasson shares this testimony:

When we moved to California from Texas in 1994, my oldest was in second grade, and it was the first time we had moved while one of the children was school-aged. Thomas did not do very well with the transition. He was a very bright child but not so good with social cues, and thus began a challenging three-year season for all of us: for Thomas as he struggled to recognize how he was antagonizing the other children, and for us as parents, as our hearts ached for his unhappiness and as we repeatedly sat through negative teacher assessments and apologized for our child's behavior.

One morning as we were all riding our bikes down to the school, it dawned on me: "I need to ask God for a scripture to hold on to for this boy so I can have hope even when things don't look good." Before I could ask, the scripture Psalm 1:3 came to mind: "He shall be like a tree planted by the rivers of water, that brings forth its fruit in its season, whose leaf also shall not wither; and whatever he does shall prosper" (NKJV). I grabbed hold of that scripture and frequently prayed that over him, especially when I was most discouraged. When our community had a fund-raiser to raise money to convert the old train station into a museum, they were selling bricks which one could have inscribed with a name or date or phrase. We purchased one and had it inscribed with Thomas's name and his Scripture verse.

Help _____ be like a tree planted by the rivers of water, that brings forth its fruit in its season, whose leaf also shall not wither; and may whatever he/she does prosper.

From Psalm 1:3 NKJV

In 1997, we moved back to Texas and I hoped that we might see a change in Thomas's school situation. Unfortunately, we began to get the same reports from teachers there. That fall, I joined a Moms in Touch group (now called Moms in Prayer) for our school and began enlisting the prayers of other moms for my child. In December of that year, as Thomas's class was celebrating a successful winter holiday program with games and refreshments, Thomas collided with another student on a small cart and was knocked to the ground, hitting his head and briefly losing consciousness. An ambulance was called, and I was notified. A quick check at the local hospital showed no signs of a concussion, and Thomas seemed fine. And suddenly, Thomas was a celebrity at the school—and not for bugging the other children. It just so happened that the next week it was his turn to be student of the week, so he received additional positive attention. We began to see a huge transformation in his behavior. At the next parent-teacher conference, his teachers marveled, saying,

"We have never seen such drastic change in a child in such a short time."

That was not the end of our challenges with Thomas. Although his interactions with the other students were no longer an issue, he continued to be the child I found myself bringing before God's throne most frequently. One sleepless night, I was up praying for him and felt like God spoke to me: "I have made him this way for a reason. You just need to help him learn to manage it." That was a huge encouragement to me. Another time, I had a dream about what he was to become. I awoke from the dream, unable to remember any of the specifics, but filled with joy at how God had worked everything together. All this time, I continued to hold onto that scripture for him.

When my husband was laid off from his job in 2002, and the only job he could find was up in Indiana, we agonized about how that move might impact Thomas, who was then just starting his junior year. We prayed and fasted about the decision, and on the third day, the day we were to give our decision about the job, I opened my Bible to where I had left off reading through Isaiah the day before and saw Isaiah 35:1-2:

> Even the wilderness and desert will be glad in those days. The wasteland will rejoice and blossom with spring crocuses. Yes, there will be an abundance of flowers and singing and joy! The deserts will become as green as the mountains of Lebanon, as lovely as Mount Carmel or the plain of Sharon. There the LORD will display his glory, the splendor of our God (NLT).

I knew that was our confirmation for my husband to take the job in Carmel, Indiana. It ended up being a wonderful opportunity for Thomas to reinvent himself at a new school and with new friends. He began really applying himself to his studies and eventually was accepted to the Air Force Academy. Basic training ended up being a really good experience for him, and we received a wonderful letter from him afterward telling us how much he now appreciated all we had done for him as parents.

In the meantime, inspired by how encouraging my Scripture verse had been to me, I encouraged the other moms in our prayer group to start off the year with what we called our "mustard seed" scripture (based on Matthew 17:20). We all prayed and identified a mountain in our child's life and chose a scripture for the year that would address that mountain. We wrote them down on 3x5 cards with a tiny mustard seed taped to it and placed them in our Bibles to remind us to pray all year long. We had our Mustard Seed Breakfast every January to celebrate what God had done in the previous year and address new mountains for the coming year. Sometimes, I shared these verses with my children, and sometimes, if they didn't ask, I just let it be between God and me.

In February of 2013, on a Saturday morning, Thomas called me from California, where he was stationed at the time, and wanted to know what his mustard seed Scripture verse was for that year. I was hesitant to tell him, because it was Proverbs 18:22: "He who finds a wife finds what is good and receives favor from the LORD." I didn't want him to feel pressured about this, so I hadn't shared it. I laughed and said, "I'm not sure I should tell you!" He laughed as well and said, "That's okay. I think I already know what it is." That scripture ended up being the confirmation he needed to proceed with courting a delightful Christian woman with whom he had been good friends for several years. As it turns out, God had spoken to that young woman's heart that same day, so Thomas's call to her later that day came as no surprise. Although we had heard about this friend, we had no idea of how they had both been seeking God and praying about this relationship. Of course, God did. And He had placed that scripture on my heart at the right time. The young couple was married not long after. We experienced great joy in remembering all the prayers on Thomas's behalf, especially seeing the fruit of years of praying with my Moms in Prayer sisters for Thomas's future spouse!

I am so thankful for God's Word and how it is something we can hold on to when things don't look like they should or how we would like them to be.

Scripture Prayers
for Building Relationships

May _____ discover how good and pleasant
it is when God's people live together in unity.

FROM PSALM 133:1

Let the peace of Christ rule in (add in the names of those in
a conflict) _____'s hearts, since as members of one
body they were called to peace. And help them be thankful.

FROM COLOSSIANS 3:15

Lord, help these momentary, light afflictions
produce in _____ an eternal weight
of glory far beyond all comparison.

FROM 2 CORINTHIANS 4:17 NASB

Help _____ understand that a gentle answer turns
away wrath, but a harsh word stirs up anger. The tongue
of the wise adorns knowledge, but the mouth of the fool
gushes folly. The soothing tongue is a tree of life, but a
perverse tongue crushes the spirit...A hot-tempered person
stirs up conflict, but the one who is patient calms a quarrel.

FROM PROVERBS 15:1-4,18

Empower _____ to be righteous, for his/
her mouth to utter wisdom, and his/her tongue
to speak what is just. May the law of God be
in his/her heart, and his/her feet not slip.

FROM PSALM 37:30-31

Encourage _____ to not become weary in doing
good, for at the proper time he/she will reap a harvest if
he/she doesn't give up. Therefore, as _____ has

opportunity, let him/her do good to all people, especially
to those who belong to the family of believers.

From Galatians 6:9-10

Lord, help _____ to have wisdom
that yields patience; remind him/her that it
is to one's glory to overlook an offense.

From Proverbs 19:11

Starting a quarrel is like breaching a dam; enable
_____ to drop the matter before a dispute breaks out.

From Proverbs 17:14

Lord, help _____ experience how
wonderful and pleasant it is when brothers
and sisters live together in harmony!

From Psalm 133:1 nlt

Help _____ not be an unfriendly person who
pursues selfish ends and against all sound judgment
starts quarrels. Fools find no pleasure in understanding
but delight in airing their own opinions. Allow
_____ to know when he/she is being foolish.

From Proverbs 18:1-2

Clothe _____ with compassion, kindness, humility,
gentleness and patience. May he/she bear with others
and forgive others. If _____ has a grievance against
someone, help him/her to forgive as You forgave him/
her. And over all these virtues help _____ put
on love, which binds us all together in perfect unity.

From Colossians 3:12-14

~

Love is patient, love is kind. It does not envy, it does not boast, it is not proud. It does not dishonor others, it is not self-seeking, it is not easily angered, it keeps no record of wrongs. Love does not delight in evil but rejoices with the truth. It always protects, always trusts, always hopes, always perseveres.

1 CORINTHIANS 13:4-7

11

Praying for Purity

*Now flee from youthful lusts and pursue
righteousness, faith, love and peace,
with those who call on the Lord from a pure heart.*

2 Timothy 2:22 NASB

A few years ago, my (Cyndie's) long-term prayer partner and I started to pray more specifically that God would safeguard our kids' brains and help them to be pure in thought, word, and action. We didn't just ask God to help them remain pure physically. But we prayed they would know their worth in Christ, "take every thought captive" (2 Corinthians 10:5 NASB), be able to "stand against the devil's schemes" (Ephesians 6:11), not be tempted beyond what they can bear (1 Corinthians 10:13), and "flee the evil desires of youth" (2 Timothy 2:22).

Starting in junior high, I was harassed by boys who thought using sexual innuendos at my expense were amusing. I felt embarrassed and disgusted, and I determined that I didn't want my children to partake in such harmful humor. That's why I began praying for purity not just in action, but also in thoughts and words. We live in a culture that is overwrought with sexuality, making it difficult to "set [our] minds on things above" (Colossians 3:2). Yet, despite the society our kids are growing up in, we can pray to a mighty God who not only hears but takes action. He can help them stand up against the devil's schemes, take every thought captive, and flee youthful lusts.

Experiencing God's Grace in Purity

My husband and I (Sally) taught our children about purity and prayed for their purity. I saw many of those prayers answered. Yet we all have free will. There are so many temptations that our children face every day, and sometimes our children will fall to temptation. God is sanctifying us, as we are not perfected yet.

Adam and Eve had the perfect parent and lived in the perfect environment, and yet they chose sin. Romans 3:23 says, "[We] all have sinned and fall short of the glory of God" (NASB). But we aren't to stay condemned. We must move to repentance, forgiveness, and walking forward with Christ. As parents, we can choose to embrace the heart of Christ, or we can become rigid, judgmental, opinionated, and ungracious people. Jesus extended grace to the person with a repentant heart. He knows the frailties of our human nature and extends grace and mercy instead of judgment. His hand is extended out, so a repentant child of God can start anew. Jesus has so much in store for our children. May we not let our frailties hinder His work.

Here is a story from a praying mom and dad: They were shocked to hear that their daughter was pregnant before marriage. The daughter handled the situation with such love, gentleness, calmness, and grace; these parents realized they needed to do the same. Their daughter chose life and marriage. And their family grew together through this time. The daughter, her child, and the marriage are precious in God's sight. Their family has blessed many. "Mercy triumphs over judgment" (James 2:13).

• •

Jesus has so much in store for our children. May we not let our frailties hinder His work.

• •

Recently, I spent time with an amazing young woman and her two-year-old daughter, Brylee. I met Stevi several years ago at church. The Lord truly shone through her. Yet, the enemy does his best to tempt us away from God's good and perfect plan. "The thief comes only to steal and kill and destroy; I [Jesus] came that they may have life, and have it abundantly" (John 10:10 NASB).

Stevi was pregnant before marriage and, instead of running away from the church, she ran to the church. And our church witnessed a miracle. Here is her story:

When we first found out we were expecting Brylee, a million thoughts crossed our minds, but a couple that stood out greater than all the rest were that God had a plan, and our church is where we would run to. David and I have attended and grown up in the same church the majority of our lives. We went to church every Sunday with our parents, and eventually the faith became ours. Since before I can remember, our young adults leader has always ingrained in those he taught how the church body is family. We are all brothers and sisters in Christ, and that overpowers any bloodline connection. Having been taught that truth early on and throughout my teen years, when things went the other direction, we knew and even told each other, "We are not going to run from Him."

I clearly remember the week we found out we were expecting. Those close to us in the church who had found out were sending us messages about how they were here for us and praying for us. There's nothing much better than opening up to those you love to tell them about a hard circumstance in your life and receiving love on the other end. It was hard to be fully known and outed as people began finding out about our pregnancy, but it built character and trust. One of the most impacting reactions was from my dad. His response was that we (the family) are going to move forward, we are going to love this baby just as much as we love all the other grandbabies, and that *all* babies are a gift. It's so true. God doesn't say that He loves those who were expected or planned; He says He loves all of His children.

When I was almost four months pregnant, David and I had our wedding. At this point, we thought we had felt all the love possible by those in the church, our family, and our circle of friends, but that was just the beginning. At 30 weeks pregnant, I went in for my second scan and discovered that a part of Brylee's brain was not showing on the ultrasound. The doctor came in to tell me that she thought something was wrong but wanted me to come back in two weeks, so she would have a different angle of her brain. I prayed the entire drive home. And so many people in our lives prayed during that two weeks of waiting. I returned to the doctor with my mom and mother-in-law, and the doctor confirmed her original beliefs, that Brylee's cavum septum pellucidum was absent. When the septum pellucidum is absent, it's a red flag for other brain anomalies. The doctor's face fell as she told me of Brylee's condition, and she repeated, "I'm sorry. I'm so sorry!" After the initial shock, the doctor told me that I was able to pursue "other options" if I pleased. Through my tears, I made known that this baby was a gift no matter how she turned out and that she was not going anywhere. As we left the office, I asked that we send a prayer request out to the church, and from that moment on I believe with my whole heart we had hundreds of people lifting our baby girl up in prayer.

The next week everything changed. I was switched to a high-risk doctor and was scheduled for a neonatal MRI to get a better look at Brylee's brain and receive a narrower diagnosis. At 33 weeks gestation, Brylee was diagnosed with bilateral schizencephaly—one closed lip and one open lip. The neurologist who read her report to us once again suggested we consider other options as this was not going to be a normal baby girl. We declined.

Brylee was born premature two weeks later, as beautiful and healthy as can be!

Here we are almost two years later with a toddler full of life, love, and a whole lot of spunk, ready to take on the world. One of my all-time favorite things is when Brylee has her neurologist appointments and we see the look on their faces when we walk into that office with our miracle baby. When Brylee's neurologist comments on how speechless she is, we let her know prayer changes things. Our God, the Greatest Physician, can work in mighty, mighty ways. Brylee certainly could have been born with all the complications her diagnosis is supposed to bring, and the best part is, He would still be faithful and just in giving us a beautiful life to love and nurture. We adore our Brylee girl, and having church family by our sides as we raise her is a joy. Our whole church body was able to pray and see the marvelous works He can do, and I couldn't be more thankful to the One we serve.

We all will fall short of His glory, but there is freedom in His name. A song that I played over and over again in my head after we found out about Brylee's diagnosis was "I Will Look Up." This song talks about how there is no one above God. As we are walking through trials, we can believe He is just, and as we come out of them, we can look back and see His faithfulness. What a beautiful picture of God it is to know that through every single circumstance, He is there, from the beginning all the way to the end. The neurologist that suggested other options at 33 weeks was right: Brylee isn't a normal little girl; she's our miracle girl!

Scripture Prayers for Purity

Strengthen _____ to put on the full armor of God,
so that he/she can take a stand against the devil's schemes.

FROM EPHESIANS 6:11

It is for freedom that Christ set _____ free.
Enable him/her to stand firm, then, and not let himself/
herself be burdened again by a yoke of slavery.

FROM GALATIANS 5:1

Not that _____ has already obtained all this, or has
already arrived at his/her goal, but help him/her press on to
take hold of that for which Christ Jesus took hold of him/
her…Help _____ do this one thing: Forgetting
what is behind and straining toward what is ahead, help
_____ press on toward the goal to win the prize for
which God has called him/her heavenward in Christ Jesus.

FROM PHILIPPIANS 3:12-14

Lord, it is Your will that _____ should be sanctified:
help him/her avoid sexual immorality and learn to
control his/her body in a way that is holy and honorable.

FROM 1 THESSALONIANS 4:3-4

Embolden _____ to flee the evil desires of youth
and pursue righteousness, faith, love and peace, along
with those who call on You out of a pure heart.

FROM 2 TIMOTHY 2:22

Empower _____ to take captive every thought
to make it obedient to Christ.

FROM 2 CORINTHIANS 10:5

Above all else, guard _____'s heart, for everything

he/she does flows from it. Keep his/her mouth free of perversity; keep corrupt talk far from his/her lips. Let his/her eyes look straight ahead; fix _____'s gaze directly before him/her. Remind him/her to give careful thought to the paths for his/her feet and be steadfast in all his/her ways. Help _____ not to turn to the right or the left, but keep his/her foot from evil.

FROM PROVERBS 4:23-27

Since _____ has been raised with Christ, help him/her set his/her heart on things above, where Christ is, seated at the right hand of God. Empower _____ to set his/her mind on things above, not on earthly things. For his/her life is now hidden with Christ in God…Help _____ put to death, therefore, whatever belongs to his/her earthly nature: sexual immorality, impurity, lust, evil desires and greed, which is idolatry.

FROM COLOSSIANS 3:1-5

Lord, help _____ forget the former things, and not dwell on the past. See, You are doing a new thing! Now it springs up. Remind _____ that you are making a way in the wilderness and streams in the wasteland.

FROM ISAIAH 43:18-19

～

You, my brothers and sisters, were called to be free.
But do not use your freedom to indulge the flesh;
rather, serve one another humbly in love.
For the entire law is fulfilled in keeping this one command:
"Love your neighbor as yourself."
If you bite and devour each other, watch out

or you will be destroyed by each other.
So I say, walk by the Spirit, and you will
not gratify the desires of the flesh.

Galatians 5:13-16

12

Praying for Boldness in Faith

Have I not commanded you? Be strong and courageous.
Do not be afraid; do not be discouraged, for the LORD
your God will be with you wherever you go.

JOSHUA 1:9

Our children can have bold faith starting at a young age and continuing through the rest of their lives. Some are called to be evangelists like my (Sally's) oldest son, Ryan, who thought street witnessing was fun. So much fun, in fact, that he made it a part of his fifteenth birthday party celebration. He and his friends ate pizza, then went to a local mall and shared about Christ. When I watch him meet someone new, in a matter of minutes he is sharing about faith in God. Both Ryan and the person listening are very happy in the conversation. Of course, not everyone is naturally bold or gifted in evangelism, but through prayer each one of us—and our kids—can become bold in our faith.

God Is for Us

In the first chapter of Joshua, we find God speaking to Joshua three times and telling him to be strong and courageous. Obviously, Joshua was afraid. But at the end of his life, he boldly proclaimed in Joshua 24:15, "But if serving the LORD seems undesirable to you, then choose for yourselves this day whom you will serve, whether the gods your ancestors served beyond the Euphrates, or the gods of the Amorites, in whose land you are living. But as for me and my household, we will serve the LORD."

Joshua learned that if God was for him, no one could stand against him. He went from fear to boldness as he placed his hope in God. As 2 Corinthians 3:12 says, "Therefore having such a hope, we use great boldness in our speech" (NASB).

Let's look at the inspiring story of David and Goliath in 1 Samuel 17. David was a youth who encountered the giant Goliath. Even the grown men of Israel fled from Goliath and were "greatly afraid" (1 Samuel 17:24 NASB). David spoke boldly to the men around him. He says in 1 Samuel 17:26, "What will be done for the man who kills this Philistine and removes this disgrace from Israel? Who is this uncircumcised Philistine that he should defy the armies of the living God?" Then he spoke boldly to Goliath:

> You come against me with sword and spear and javelin, but I come against you in the name of the LORD Almighty, the God of the armies of Israel, whom you have defied. This day the LORD will deliver you into my hands, and I'll strike you down and cut off your head. This very day I will give the carcasses of the Philistine army to the birds and the wild animals, and the whole world will know that there is a God in Israel (1 Samuel 17:45-46).

You probably know the end of this story, which is summed up in 1 Samuel 17:50, "So David triumphed over the Philistine with a sling and a stone; without a sword in his hand he struck down the Philistine and killed him."

There are many different types of giants that can come into our children's lives: school, social media, bullies, fears, mental health, temptations, diseases, divorce, loss of a loved one, etc. Just as Joshua and David became bold and conquered giants and enemies, our children can be bold in their faith and defeat all that comes their way.

First, we must boldly and confidently pray for them.

Hebrews 4:16 says, "So let us come boldly to the very throne of God and stay there to receive his mercy and to find grace to help us in our times of need" (TLB). With every prayer, our children can become like Paul, Mary, Deborah, Daniel, Joshua, David, and others who stood boldly in the power of the Holy Spirit. Go through the Bible and read about your favorite heroes of the faith and pray verses from these stories over your children.

....

Just as Joshua and David became bold and conquered giants and enemies, our children can be bold in their faith and defeat all that comes their way.

....

We know that as their faith grows, they will become bold. "So faith comes from hearing, and hearing by the word of Christ," Romans 10:17 (NASB). As they spend time with God, their hearts will be transformed from fear to boldness. Second Corinthians 3:18 says, "But we all, with unveiled face, beholding as in a mirror the glory of the Lord, are being transformed into the same image from glory to glory, just as from the Lord, the Spirit" (NASB).

Joy Moreau, a Moms in Prayer leader, shares this testimony:

We prayed Philippians 2:15-16 for our children: *That _____ will live a clean, innocent life as a child of God in a dark world full of people who are crooked and stubborn. That he/she will shine out among them like a beacon light, holding out to them the Word of Life* (TLB). Here's how God answered:

When our son Mitchell was in kindergarten, he shared the plan of salvation with the students in his class during the sharing time. His teacher told me how he knew the steps to life with Christ and told the students in his class.

In the fifth grade, Mitchell was in a class where they were having a writing competition. The students were to write about a family treasure. It was due on the Monday after Mother's Day. On Mother's Day, a local paper featured an interview with me about Moms in Prayer, prompting Mitchell to write about me and what we do in this ministry. His paper won for his class. Each classroom winner was given the opportunity to read their paper to all the parents who had children who had won in their classroom. I attended to hear the stories, as did many others. The room was packed full of parents, and they heard Mitchell share about Moms in Prayer and the treasure of praying for children and schools.

That same year Mitchell's class had a project to write about someone and then play that person in a living museum. Mitchell chose Billy Graham and wrote about how he preached the Bible. He also recorded some messages from the Billy Graham Crusades and had those playing as he told about this godly man from North Carolina teaching the Bible all over the world. Every student in the school came through the library to hear these presentations.

I thank God for hearing this prayer and allowing my son to hold out to them the Word of Life. To God be the glory.

Now it's your turn. Your child might not have the spiritual gift of evangelism, but we can pray that each one of our kids will have the boldness to share Christ's love with others and that Christ would shine through them like a beacon, attracting those around them to the Word of Life.

Scripture Prayers for Boldness in Faith

Lord, enable _____ to be strong and
courageous. Help him/her to not be afraid and
to not be discouraged, for the Lord our God
will be with him/her wherever he/she goes.

FROM JOSHUA 1:9

Empower _____ to let his/her light shine
before others, that they may see his/her good
deeds and glorify You, Father, in heaven.

FROM MATTHEW 5:6

Inspire _____ to preach the word; to be prepared
in season and out of season; to correct, rebuke, and
encourage—with great patience and careful instruction.

FROM 2 TIMOTHY 4:2

Lord, encourage _____ to choose for himself/
herself this day whom he/she will serve…May he/
she and his/her household serve the Lord.

FROM JOSHUA 24:15

Lord, help _____ proclaim the kingdom
of God and teach about the Lord Jesus Christ—
with all boldness and without hindrance!

FROM ACTS 28:31

Therefore having such a hope, help _____
use great boldness in his/her speech.

FROM 2 CORINTHIANS 3:12 NASB

In _____'s heart may he/she revere You as
Lord, and always be prepared to give an answer to
everyone who asks him/her to give the reason for the

hope that he/she has. Help _____ do this with gentleness and respect, keeping a clear conscience, so that those who speak maliciously against his/her good behavior in Christ may be ashamed of their slander.

FROM 1 PETER 3:15-16

Let _____ come boldly to the very throne of God and stay there to receive Your mercy and to find grace to help in his/her times of need.

FROM HEBREWS 4:16 TLB

Remind _____ that he/she can do all things through You, Lord, who strengthens him/her.

FROM PHILIPPIANS 4:13

Help _____ live a clean, innocent life as a child of God in a dark world full of people who are crooked and stubborn. Help him/her shine out among them like a beacon light, holding out to them the Word of Life.

FROM PHILIPPIANS 2:15-16 TLB

❧

I love you, LORD, my strength.

The LORD is my rock, my fortress and my deliverer;
      my God is my rock, in whom I take refuge,
      my shield and the horn of my salvation,
      my stronghold.
I called to the LORD, who is worthy of praise,
      and I have been saved from my enemies.
The cords of death entangled me;
      the torrents of destruction overwhelmed me.
The cords of the grave coiled around me;

the snares of death confronted me.
In my distress I called to the LORD;
I cried to my God for help.
From his temple he heard my voice;
my cry came before him, into his ears...

As for God, his way is perfect:
The LORD's word is flawless;
he shields all who take refuge in him.
For who is God besides the LORD?
And who is the Rock except our God?
It is God who arms me with strength
and keeps my way secure.
He makes my feet like the feet of a deer;
he causes me to stand on the heights.
He trains my hands for battle;
my arms can bend a bow of bronze.
You make your saving help my shield,
and your right hand sustains me;
your help has made me great.
You provide a broad path for my feet,
so that my ankles do not give way...

The LORD lives! Praise be to my Rock!
Exalted be God my Savior!

PSALM 18:1-6,30-36,46

13

Praying for Our Children's Future

*Trust in the LORD with all your heart; do not depend
on your own understanding. Seek his will in all you
do, and he will show you which path to take.*

PROVERBS 3:5-6 NLT

I (Cyndie) dropped off my son at the train station early one
morning so he could meet his friend in Los Angeles to film a pro-
motional piece for their short film. Once I got home, I happily sat
down in my comfy, red quiet-time chair for some moments with
the Lord. I was turning pages to resume my reading and medita-
tion on 2 Timothy, but before I could get back to that passage, God
stopped me in the Psalms—Psalm 20, to be exact. There was a well-
worn passage, where I had written dates when I had prayed the passage for others or claimed it for myself. I had forgotten that just a
few months before, I had written "For my graduates," as my son was
graduating from college and my daughter from high school.

What a privilege to have been praying all these years for my children's futures, and here they were living out all those answers to
so many prayers. This passage drove home a powerful moment of
reflection and thanksgiving for all God has done already—and for
all that I know God has planned for my kids in the future—plans
to align their desires with His and make their plans succeed for His
glory and purpose.

Psalm 20:1-2,4-5

> May the LORD answer you when you are in distress;
>   may the name of the God of Jacob protect you.
> May he send you help from the sanctuary
>   and grant you support...
>
> May he give you the desire of your heart
>   and make all your plans succeed.
> May we shout for joy over your victory
>   and lift up our banners in the name of our God.

During my quiet time, I praised God for being our protector, I confessed my parental worries, and I began thanking Him for carrying my kids through their school years. In *Unshaken* I share some of the heart-wrenching difficulties both of my kids experienced. Yet, God has been adding the exclamation points of life by giving them the desires of their hearts and making their plans succeed—not always as we want, but in ways that we can trust that God's working out a good plan for their lives.

I took a picture of the verses and texted it to Elliott, who replied, "That's perfect!"

Since he was preschool age, he wanted to be a filmmaker. He began winning awards for his short films in eighth grade and, with the grace of God, has continued to find success in the field of work that God put on his heart early. Now, here is a college graduate ready to launch into the "real world" of full-time work, paying rent, driving through treacherous southern California traffic, and figuring out this "adulting" thing.

So I prayed this for both of my kids:

Lord, give Elliott and Zoe the desires of their heart and make their plans succeed, so we will shout for joy over the victory you've given them and wave our joyous banners excitedly in the name of Jesus Christ. And when my heart goes to fear that Satan will pull them away or that their success will be a long time in coming, I pray the beginning of those verses that God will answer them when they are in distress, that the God of Jacob will protect them, and that He will send them help from His sanctuary and grant them support.

What propels me forward in my fervent prayers on days when God's purpose isn't clear or His path easily detected? Remembering what God has done in the past. Elliott has struggled with dyslexia over the years, yet he just graduated from college magna cum laude in four years, earning the respect of his peers and teachers. As we prayed for his perseverance, God granted it in spades. I started my first Moms in Prayer group when Elliott was in second grade and was already struggling with two-dimensional schoolwork like worksheets and reading. I remember wondering back then if he'd even graduate from high school.

What a joy to look back over the many years of praying for his future—of all the heartache and prayers for direction—to walk the joyful journey of witnessing the fruit of all those answers to prayer. Are we finished praying now that he's a college graduate? Of course not. We will continue to intercede on his behalf, asking God to show him the good purposes for which he was created (Ephesians 2:10).

> Lord, help _____ know that he/she is Your
> handiwork, created in Christ Jesus to do good works,
> which God prepared in advance for him/her to do.
>
> FROM EPHESIANS 2:10

Praying When the Path Is Unclear

Now, I know that in the middle of struggles it can be difficult to pray for perseverance with wholehearted conviction, especially when one's heart is breaking. God has been especially testing us through my daughter's continuous bouts with injuries that sideline her from her passion of dancing and her desire to be a dance coach to mentor and train teens. Yet, year after year come the injuries—injuries that have yet to sideline her dreams.

She's broken a piece of her spine, had knee surgery—both of which God healed quickly. But the injury in her final senior year of dance competitions has been a hard one to wrap our brains around, because it has raised a big ol' stop sign at seemingly every turn.

When she started her freshman year in high school, she was involved in an array of extracurricular activities: musical theater, gymnastics, school choir, singing in worship bands, helping with kids choir, teaching on Sundays. And, because we knew and adored the dance teacher and coach of the brand-new competitive dance team at the charter high school she attended, she also joined the dance team. She loved dance as a tiny tyke, with her cute, messy ponytails and serious expression, trying to be ever so precise. She continued through fifth grade, before moving on to gymnastics. As my Moms in Prayer group prayed for her to find her passion and purpose, the other interests subsided and what was left was a passion for not just dance but for the beautiful, artistic expression of choreography and encouraging her teammates. And she developed a skill I didn't realize she had: the uncanny ability to squash teenage drama. Not all of the drama, of course—only Jesus Christ Himself can soften the hormonal punctuations that infuse high school drama. Soon her future career goal was to become a high school dance teacher and coach.

During her junior year, she injured her knee, and we scheduled surgery so it would have the least impact on her tryouts for the competition dance pieces and her audition for the college dance team. The surgery went well. She healed up quickly, performing many dances for the Christmas performance at school. The competition season started well. Her dance solo scores began to climb. As God had arranged it, the two dance nationals that usually land on the same weekends were separated by a week. Zoe performed her solo at the first dance nationals and won thirteenth place. She felt she could do better, so she pushed herself to be ready for the following nationals. For over a month, no matter what we were praying for, she'd end the prayer with "and I pray that we win a championship banner and backpacks at nationals." The five-year-old team had never won a first place at nationals, and she really wanted that banner for the school's assembly area and championship backpacks for her team.

I drove some of the dancers to the competition. As we began the trek from San Diego to Orange County on the notoriously trafficked I-5 in California, a digital street sign warned of an impending storm. The rain started just as my 3:20 alarm went off, reminding me to pray Ephesians 3:20 prayers—that God would answer in ways that are more than all we ask or imagine. I prayed that God would hold off the rain temporarily so we could arrive safely (which He did!) and that the girls would do well in their competition.

At the first nationals, we were ecstatic that the small jazz number Zoe was in with four other girls won first place in their category, taking home a nationals banner—and nationals jackets. That became a well-worn, prized possession of the girls in that number, and especially the seniors. The following week was the second nationals—the "real" nationals for Zoe and her friend who had been on the team all four years.

Zoe's solo was the team's first dance of the three-day USA dance competition. She was ready and eager to "leave it all on the floor." She hadn't felt like she had done her best run yet, and that was her goal. Her teammates and I lined up to cheer her on. She stepped out on the floor and brought it. Her piece was moving, and her emotional expressions mirrored the deep expressions of the music and the choreography. She was just 30 seconds into the piece when she went into her leap—a beautiful leap she had performed dozens of times, but this time was different. There was an unmistakable pop sound. She went into the next formation, but as she tried to come back down on her right foot, she stopped. I held my breath as the coach ran onto the floor. My daughter who lived out the hashtag #nevertoosickorbrokentoperform hopped off the dance floor, leaning on her coach. Zoe's only concern was being able to finish her dance solo. They bandaged her up, but since she couldn't put weight on it, they sent her for an X-ray.

While I like to think that I'm good in a crisis, at that moment my brain froze. But God lovingly had the dance coach, assistant coach, and our dear friends there to guide us to each next step. The Ramoses, our friends since our girls began kindergarten together, kindly drove us to the ER and waited for the X-ray and tentative diagnosis of "just a sprain." The doctor cautioned Zoe not to dance the rest of the weekend so she could audition for the college dance team the following weekend. What a horrible choice!

The next morning as we ate breakfast with the team, my usually strong daughter cried as her coach asked how she was doing. She was devastated, but she stayed upbeat for her team, helping train different dancers to fill in for her in their group pieces. My heart ached for her as she watched the girls perform without her. I found my heart praying, "Blessed is the one who perseveres under trial because, having stood the test, that person will receive the crown of life that the Lord has promised to those who love him" (James 1:12).

> Blessed is _____ who perseveres under trial because, having stood the test, _____ will receive the crown of life that You, Lord, promised to those who love You.
>
> FROM JAMES 1:12

And, on the final night, God answered her month-long prayer: They shocked all of us by taking the win for their large jazz number, earning a championship banner for the school and backpacks for all of them. Later, I joked with Zoe that her prayer wasn't specific enough. When she prayed her team would win championship backpacks, she hadn't actually prayed that she would be dancing with her teammates!

She was devastated to miss dancing at her last nationals. And we were even more devastated to hear from our family doctor and then orthopedic doctor there was no way she'd be auditioning for the college dance team the following weekend. Unfortunately, she was still injured and couldn't dance for the other possible college dance scholarship either. It was both a financial hit as well as the death of a dream. I have since prayed Psalm 18 for her a lot.

Psalm 18:32-36

> It is God who arms me with strength
> > and keeps my way secure.
> He makes my feet like the feet of a deer;
> > he causes me to stand on the heights.
> He trains my hands for battle;
> > my arms can bend a bow of bronze.
> You make your saving help my shield,
> > and your right hand sustains me;
> > your help has made me great.
> You provide a broad path for my feet,
> > so that my ankles do not give way.

And when I saw the gorgeous photos of her dancing, I purchased all of them, and on the picture of the leap, I added the verses from Isaiah 40:28-31:

> Do you not know?
> > Have you not heard?
> The Lord is the everlasting God,
> > the Creator of the ends of the earth.
> He will not grow tired or weary,
> > and his understanding no one can fathom.
> He gives strength to the weary
> > and increases the power of the weak.

Even youths grow tired and weary,
    and young men stumble and fall;
but those who hope in the Lord
    will renew their strength.
They will soar on wings like eagles;
    they will run and not grow weary,
    they will walk and not be faint.

We prayed the college dance team would have a second audition—and they did! However, it was exactly when her final high school spring dance concert was, and she didn't want to miss dancing with her team one last time. Either way, the week of both events, the orthopedic doctor cautioned her not to dance. As we drove home from the appointment, I asked her what she was going to do about the concert. "I'm going to dance," she said with determination. "Maybe you could take yourself out of some of the numbers," I suggested. But I have long since learned I'm not my children's Holy Spirit, and so I prayed God would give her wisdom. And despite the tears and frustrations—and the fact she hadn't danced for six weeks—she performed beautifully. She had some pain, but much less than I had anticipated. She choreographed several numbers, sang a beautiful solo, and danced 18 numbers between the two shows. God allowed her to have her big high school finale, surrounded by the teammates she adored.

Unfortunately, during the summer, an MRI showed that she had injured her cartilage, which was causing the pain. She was put back in a walking boot right before starting her freshman year of college and had to drop the dance classes she had been happily anticipating. Zoe occasionally asks why God would let this happen. The answer: I have no idea. But the timing was so perfectly imperfect that we know God is up to something. All we can do is pray and trust that He is shaping her future for His best plan. Someday we will look back on the dashed dreams and see the beautiful plan God was unfolding for her life. Until then, we hold on to the hope of Romans

8:28, "And we know that in all things God works for the good of those who love him, who have been called according to his purpose."

Lord, help _____ know that in all things You
work for the good of those who love You, who
have been called according to Your purpose.

FROM ROMANS 8:28

Holding Out Hope

While we wait for God to finish writing the rest of my daughter's story, be encouraged with these two testimonies. The first one is from longtime Moms in Prayer leader Debbie Strobel.

My most memorable event concerning scripture prayer happened in the fall of '07 and winter of '08. My oldest son, Preston, had always dreamed of attending the U.S. Coast Guard Academy, but we knew it would be extremely difficult to get in as they only accept about ten percent of those who apply. We were waiting to hear if he received early admission when God spoke to me through our Moms in Prayer group. I had chosen *hope* as our attribute for which to praise God and was reading from Lamentations 3:21-26. But the word that jumped out at me several times from the passage was *wait*. I had a feeling that God was telling me that my son would not get early admission and would have to "wait quietly" (verse 26). That very afternoon he received a letter stating that his early admission application was denied, and he would be put into the regular admission process. So, we waited.

In February of '08 the attribute I had chosen for our group that morning was God as the Revealer. As we praised Him for that attribute, I sensed He was telling me Preston's appointment would be revealed. That very afternoon Preston received a call from an admission officer telling him that he was accepted. Usually they just send out a letter, but instead she chose to let him know early with a personal call.

I kept a scrapbook of his time at the academy, and two pages are those two letters (the bad and the good) and the verses through which God spoke. Preston will always have that as a memorial stone showing God's faithfulness.

In 2011, during a visit to the Academy, I found out an amazing addition to this story. They told me that only a handful of those denied early admission are later accepted into the Academy!

Praying for a Future Spouse

Almost nothing impacts our children's future as much as their choice of a spouse. That's why in Moms in Prayer we encourage groups to occasionally pray that God will be preparing a godly spouse who complements their child so they can serve the Lord together. In a previous chapter, we shared one of these answers to prayers. Here is another one:

As we pray in our Moms in Prayer groups, God answers in amazing ways. One way to encourage each other is to share these great stories. If you are a mom with young children, or any age child who is not married, one of the main things you might be praying for is for God to bring them a godly spouse who will be their partner for life. That prayer was answered for me on December 30, 2017, when my oldest son, Preston, married Alla.

The fact that they were even able to find each other is truly a God-story! Alla was born in Iran to Muslim parents. Her dad, Hamid, was a soldier who got severely injured in the Iran-Iraq War, so he left the military and began importing goods from the Ukraine. On one of his visits there, a friend invited him to visit a Christian church, where he was given a Bible in his own language and was challenged by the pastor to read the Gospel of John. He took the Bible and began reading it along with his Koran, assuming he would find it worthless. But as he read both books, he ended up holding the Bible in his hand and proclaiming, "This is the truth!" Because of his new faith, he was not allowed to return to Iran. Eventually, he was able to bring his family to the Ukraine, where they lived for several years before immigrating to the United States with the help of an American church.

Seven years later, Alla met my son in San Diego, and they were married about 18 months after that. The day I began praying for Preston's future spouse when he was just a child, I could never have imagined that God would orchestrate all these circumstances to get his perfect mate to him.

Scripture Prayers for the Future

Lord, thank You that You know the plans You have
for _____, plans to prosper and not harm him/
her, plans to give _____ hope and a future.

FROM JEREMIAH 29:11

Lord, remind _____ that there is no wisdom,
no insight, no plan that can succeed against the Lord.

FROM PROVERBS 21:30

Lord, help _____ know that in all things
You work for the good of those who love You, who
have been called according to Your purpose.

FROM ROMANS 8:28

Help _____ not throw away his/her confidence;
it will be richly rewarded. _____ needs to
persevere so that when he/she has done the will of
God, he/she will receive what You have promised.

FROM HEBREWS 10:35-36

Show _____ your ways, Lord, teach him/
her Your paths. Guide _____ in Your
truth and teach him/her, for You are God my
Savior, and my hope is in You all day long.

FROM PSALM 25:4-5

Whether _____ turns to the right
or to the left, allow him/her to clearly hear
You say, "This is the way; walk in it."

FROM ISAIAH 30:21

To humans belong the plans of the heart, but from
You, Lord, comes the proper answer of the tongue.

All our ways seem pure to us, but You weigh our
motives. Help _____ commit to You whatever
he/she does, so You will establish his/her plans.

FROM PROVERBS 16:1-3

May _____ call on You, God, for
You will answer him/her; turn Your ear to
_____ and hear his/her prayer.

FROM PSALM 17:6

Let love and faithfulness never leave _____;
bind them around his/her neck, write them on the
tablet of his/her heart. Then _____ will win
favor and a good name in the sight of God and man.

FROM PROVERBS 3:3-4

Help _____ trust in You, Lord, with all his/her
heart and not depend on his/her own understanding.
Remind him/her to seek Your will in all he/she does and
show him/her which path to take. May _____
not be impressed with his/her own wisdom, but
instead fear the Lord and turn away from evil.

FROM PROVERBS 3:5-7 NLT

Grant _____ his/her heart's desires and
make all his/her plans succeed. May we shout for
joy when we hear of his/her victory and raise a
victory banner in the name of You, our God. Lord,
we ask that You answer all his/her prayers.

FROM PSALM 20:4-5 NLT

A Special Prayer for Christians

Let _____ hear of Your unfailing love each morning,
for he/she is trusting You. Show _____ where
to walk, for he/she gives himself/herself to You. Rescue
_____ from his/her enemies, Lord; he/she runs

to You to hide. Teach _____ to do Your will, for You are his/her God. May Your gracious Spirit lead him/her forward on a firm footing. For the glory of Your name, O Lord, preserve his/her life. Because of Your faithfulness, bring _____ out of this distress.

Psalm 143:8-11 nlt

～

Yet this I call to mind and therefore I have hope:
Because of the Lord's great love we are not consumed,
for his compassions never fail.
They are new every morning; great is your faithfulness.
I say to myself, "The Lord is my portion;
therefore I will wait for him."
The Lord is good to those whose hope is in him,
to the one who seeks him;
it is good to wait quietly for the salvation of the Lord."

Lamentations 3:21-26

14

Praying for the Teachers, Coaches, and Mentors in Their Lives

Be shepherds of God's flock that is under your care, watching over them—not because you must, but because you are willing, as God wants you to be; not pursuing dishonest gain, but eager to serve; not lording it over those entrusted to you, but being examples to the flock. And when the Chief Shepherd appears, you will receive the crown of glory that will never fade away.

1 PETER 5:2-4

More than likely, you are not the only adult influencing your child. Teachers, coaches, ministers, counselors, and mentors can have a profound impact on the lives of a child. Think of the coach screaming at the little tykes on the soccer field who can't figure out which goal is theirs. What impact does that have on the kids—and on the family? On the other hand, think of the loving coach who pushes your child to persevere, to give "a little more," to work as a team player and help create unity. Teachers and coaches not only guide our children to develop physical and academic skills but also character traits that influence who your child is and how he or she will develop.

As mentioned in the previous chapter, my (Cyndie's) daughter, Zoe, tried a variety of extracurricular activities when she entered high school. The one she fell in love with was the one that offered the most challenge. She grew in her skills and strength so she could make her high school dance teacher and team proud. Her teacher challenged them to be their best, but if a performance didn't go well, she'd shrug it off and say, "That's okay." What was striking was that the teacher—who had spent most of her life working within the competitive dance world—never took it personally or interpreted a win or disappointment as a reflection on herself. I was always impressed with that. She demanded good behavior and good teamwork, and my daughter continues to grow as a person under her leadership and mentoring.

On the other hand, a difficult teacher or coach can make the year extremely long. So, in either case, let's remember to pray for the adults in our children's lives, whether it's a teacher, coach, youth pastor, mentor, principal, school counselor, or maybe even the school security guard, lunch lady, or nurse.

Ty Nichols, a coach and son of Moms in Prayer international founder Fern Nichols, told a group of moms, "A fervent praying warrior goes to battle for me each day. Isn't that sweet? She picks up her sword and her shield, and she goes to work! I'm a coach, and I understand what that means—to sweat and bleed, and rough it out; and you do that every time you pray. This isn't tiddlywinks, and it's not patty-cake. This is war, and you're going to war on behalf of your kids."

When We Pray for Teachers, We Impact the Future!

You and I have the great privilege and opportunity to pray for teachers. They will impact the children and the school in big and small ways. Our prayers can bring salvation to those who do not know Him. Many times, I (Sally) have witnessed salvation happen for teachers and staff. We must stand in the gap for teachers who know Jesus. Our prayers will bring blessings, success, wisdom, protection, peace, joy, and so much more. Below is a testimony from one of those amazing teachers, Cathy Bamber. Prayer empowers those you pray for!

He entered my classroom slowly and a little unsurely. I already knew who he was and knew he needed extra time and extra patience, based on what his teacher from the previous year had told me. I was ready...I thought.

Alongside this young man was his mom. I would soon learn that she was also his cheerleader. His biggest fan. His hope.

She and I got to know each other quickly as we met to discuss his daily challenges. Never did she criticize my methods. On the contrary, she would bring me little notes and small gifts. Her words included things like, "You are making a difference," "You are making each child feel special," "You are a blessing." I was overwhelmed by these gestures of kindness.

She told me that she knew God had a plan for his life. She asked me to be patient in believing.

I believed right alongside her.

This mom displayed trust in me. She told me she was praying for me! She was one of the Moms in Prayer moms who prayed for our school, my class, and her son. My heart softened even more toward this child. I envisioned this mom standing over her child's bed in the wee hours, praying he would be all God wanted him to be, knowing that God, who began a good work in him, would be faithful to complete it until the day of Christ (Philippians 1:6). Each morning before school, I would stand over his chair and pray for him. "God, help him to have peace today. Help him to obey. Help him to have friends. Give me wisdom in reaching him."

Remember how I thought I was ready for this student to be in my class that year? I had no idea what God would do in me through that praying mom. As I look back on that year, I remember the impact she had on me. She could have challenged my ways. She could have criticized me. She could have been unsupportive. But instead, she chose to demonstrate love and faith. She prayed for me. Just like Jesus.

Moms, whether your child's teacher is a believer or not, always know that God is working through your faithful prayers and that the Great Intercessor, Jesus, will be pleading to the Father for your child as well (Romans 8:34). You and Jesus, what a team! "The Lord Himself goes before [your child and]...will never leave [them] nor forsake [them]" (Deuteronomy 31:8).

Go forth with godly love, deep faith, and sincere humility, and the Lord will work in ways you would never imagine.

••

Always know that the Great Intercessor, Jesus, will be pleading to the Father for your child.

••

Parents, are you struggling with the idea that your child has a difficult teacher or coach or other adult in his/her life? Start praying! And don't just pray for your child to grow, develop, and persevere through the struggle; also pray for the difficult adults. Pray that those adults will come to a wholehearted relationship with Jesus Christ. Pray they will have "ears to hear and eyes to see" and that God will grant them insight, wisdom, and a contagious joy. Pray that God brings them clarity and peace for whatever is happening in their home life that could be causing the stress that is overflowing into the classroom. Pray and watch as God impacts not only that teacher/coach but also the class/team.

Scripture Prayers for Teachers and School Staff

Give _____ wisdom and knowledge, and help _____ be strong and courageous, because he/she will lead these people.

FROM 2 CHRONICLES 1:10 AND JOSHUA 1:6

Lord, urge _____ to warn those who are idle and disruptive, encourage the disheartened, help the weak, and be patient with everyone.

FROM 1 THESSALONIANS 5:14

Enable _____ to correct, rebuke, and encourage— with great patience and careful instruction.

FROM 2 TIMOTHY 4:2-5

Lord, help _____ to follow these proverbs: "The wise in heart are called discerning, and gracious words promote instruction. Prudence is a fountain of life to the prudent, but folly brings punishment to fools. The hearts of the wise make their mouths prudent, and their lips promote instruction. Gracious words are a honeycomb, sweet to the soul and healing to the bones."

FROM PROVERBS 16:21-24

Help _____ instruct the wise and they will be wiser still; teach the righteous and they will add to their learning.

FROM PROVERBS 9:9

Help _____ devote himself/herself to prayer, being watchful and thankful.

FROM COLOSSIANS 4:2

Lord, whatever _____ does, may he/she work
heartily as for the Lord rather than for men.

From Colossians 3:23 nasb

May _____ not become weary in doing
good, for at the proper time, _____ will
reap a harvest if he/she does not give up.

From Galatians 6:9

Lord, I pray that _____ will
trust in You and do good.

From Psalm 37:3

Lord, may integrity and honesty protect
_____ as he/she puts his/her hope in You.

From Psalm 25:21 nlt

Lord, may _____ take joy in doing Your will.
May Your instructions be written on his/her heart.

From Psalm 40:8 nlt

May _____ not follow the advice of the wicked,
or stand around with sinners, or join in with mockers.

From Psalm 1:1 nlt

Lord, I pray that _____ will love your
instructions, have great peace, and not stumble.

From Psalm 119:165 nlt

∽

*I pray that out of his glorious riches he may strengthen you
with power through his Spirit in your inner being,
so that Christ may dwell in your hearts through faith.*

And I pray that you, being rooted and established in love,
may have power, together with all the Lord's holy people,
to grasp how wide and long and high and deep is the love
of Christ, and to know this love
that surpasses knowledge—that you may be filled
to the measure of all the fullness of God.

Ephesians 3:16-19

Part III

Encouraging the Legacy of Prayer

15

Praying This Generation Will Impact Others for Christ

We will not hide them from their descendants;
we will tell the next generation
the praiseworthy deeds of the LORD,
his power, and the wonders he has done.
He decreed statutes for Jacob
and established the law in Israel,
which he commanded our ancestors
to teach their children,
so the next generation would know them,
even the children yet to be born,
and they in turn would tell their children.
Then they would put their trust in God
and would not forget his deeds
but would keep his commands.

PSALM 78:4-7

I (Sally) have good news for you, news that will give you hope! As I travel around the world, I am witnessing God raise up a mighty generation—a generation like no other. They are bold and fearless for the things of God. God is hearing and answering our prayers for this generation.

Listen, dear friends, God did not make a mistake when He chose your children to be born in this period of time. He chose them specifically for right here and right now, and with their talents, circumstances, and walk to impact this world for Christ. His desire is to work through them powerfully. So, we must be praying for them! The enemy would love to destroy this generation or discourage them. Satan's desire is that they be "a stubborn and rebellious generation, a generation that did not prepare its heart and whose spirit was not faithful to God" (Psalm 78:8 NASB). And yet God tells us in 1 Corinthians 2:9, "However, as it is written: 'What no eye has seen, what no ear has heard, and what no human mind has conceived'—the things God has prepared for those who love him."

* *

God did not make a mistake when He chose your children to be born in this period of time...to impact this world for Christ.

* *

What God wants to do here on the earth, He will do through intercessors—those who will stand in the gap for this generation. When God wants to bring change to our sinful world, He looks for an intercessor on which He can place His desires. He has the power to raise up the greatest generation the world has ever seen.

God Is Working Through This Generation

You may have read in our book *Unshaken* the story of my youngest daughter's high school, where we prayed our children would rise up and impact others for Christ. We prayed Psalm 78:6-7 and many other scriptures. She and her friends started a Bible study in the evening so others could join in, and they too prayed as their moms did that revival and spiritual awakening would happen on their campus. God answered. And 91 students gave their lives to Jesus, and some rededicated their lives back to Him! As the school year progressed, others surrendered their hearts to Jesus. My daughter recently discovered that, many years later, this student-led Bible study is still happening.

My daughter began helping at her church with high school students. She started leading a team for the high school youth group to pray scriptures over the students. The high school group grew from 50 students to 120 students. Since the beginning of the school year, 50 of those students have been baptized, witnessing to the world that they are followers of Christ. The pastor, seeing this, asked my daughter to be the prayer leader for the whole church. Keep praying for this generation, my friends. God is working powerfully.

Megan Callendar, a child of a prayer warrior, writes:

> My mom's prayers are commissioning me, and prayer is the place where that happens! Because she has brought my name before God over and over, He has provided direction for my life. His favor has followed me to every place I have gone, and He has given me great and precious promises to hold on to through trials. My mom's prayers have had a sharpening effect on my life, giving me a deep love for Jesus, a heart yielded to His will, and a burden to share my faith with those who are lost.

Nick Hall, founder of PULSE and an evangelistic voice for the next generation, was prayed for by his mom who prayed Scripture over him. During college he was impacting his campus for Christ. To this day he is still impacting college campuses, sometimes bringing over 60,000 college students together to worship God and seeing thousands of them come to Christ.

What will God do as we pray Scripture for this generation? What will happen when we raise up these kids and young adults in prayer to impact the next generation for Christ? Amazing things that only God can plan and manifest. What happened to the generation after Moses—the generation after the ones who were so fearful that they refused to enter the promised land and remained in the harsh desert instead? God appointed Joshua to lead that new generation into the promised land. That generation of Israelites was victorious, making the land they lived in a place where God was worshipped and obeyed. As we pray for this generation using scriptures, they, too, will be victorious. Let's pray for this generation to rise up together to impact their cities, nations, and the world with the love of Christ.

Scripture Prayers
for the Next Generation

Lord, we cry out on behalf of today's children, teens, and young adults. May they know therefore that the Lord our God is God; that You are the faithful God, keeping Your covenant of love to a thousand generations of those who love You and keep Your commandments.

FROM DEUTERONOMY 7:9

Lord, may Your plans stand firm forever, the purposes of Your heart through all generations.

FROM PSALM 33:11

Lord, we cry out for today's youngest generation that they will shout for joy to the Lord in all the earth. That they will worship You, Lord, with gladness and come before You with joyful songs. May they know that You, Lord, are God, and it is You who made us, and we are Yours; we are Your people, the sheep of Your pasture. May they enter Your gates with thanksgiving and Your courts with praise. May they give You thanks and praise Your name. For You, Lord, are good and Your love endures forever; Your faithfulness continues through all generations.

FROM PSALM 100:1-5

Therefore, since we are surrounded by such a great cloud of witnesses, let this next generation throw off everything that hinders and the sin that so easily entangles. And let them run with perseverance the race marked out for them, fixing their eyes on Jesus, the pioneer and perfecter of faith. For the joy set before Him, He endured the cross, scorning its shame, and sat down at the right hand of the throne of God. May this younger generation

consider Him who endured such opposition from
sinners, so that they will not grow weary and lose heart.

FROM HEBREWS 12:1-3

Have mercy on this generation, O God, have mercy!
May they look to You for protection. May they hide
beneath the shadow of Your wings until the danger
passes by. Remind them to cry out to God Most
High, to God who will fulfill His purpose for them.

FROM PSALM 57:1-2 NLT

Scripture Prayers for Individuals of This Next Generation

Empower _____ to not be conformed to this world but be transformed by the renewing of his/her mind, so that _____ may prove what the will of God is, that which is good and acceptable and perfect.

FROM ROMANS 12:2 NASB

May _____ know that the Lord our God, the Lord is one. May he/she love the Lord God with all his/her heart and with all his/her soul and with all his/her strength. May Your commandments be on his/her heart. May he/she impress them on his/her children.

FROM DEUTERONOMY 6:4-7

Lord, help _____ prove to be blameless and innocent, a child of God above reproach in the midst of a crooked and perverse generation, among whom he/she can appear as a light in the world.

FROM PHILIPPIANS 2:15 NASB

Encourage _____ to go forth clothed with power from on high.

FROM LUKE 24:49

May _____ receive power as the Holy Spirit comes on him/her; and may _____ be your witness in Jerusalem, and in all Judea and Samaria, and to the ends of the earth.

FROM ACTS 1:8

~

I am the vine; you are the branches.
If you remain in me and I in you, you will bear much fruit;
apart from me you can do nothing.
If you do not remain in me,
you are like a branch that is thrown away and withers;
such branches are picked up,
thrown into the fire and burned.
If you remain in me and my words remain in you,
ask whatever you wish, and it will be done for you.
This is to my Father's glory, that you bear much fruit,
showing yourselves to be my disciple.

JOHN 15:5-8

16

Teaching Children to Pray

One generation commends your works to another;
they tell of your mighty acts.
They speak of the glorious splendor of your majesty—
and I will meditate on your wonderful works.

Psalm 145:4-5

When my (Cyndie's) kids were little, I had the privilege of praying the four steps of prayer with them when we had leisure summer mornings. I'd share a verse with an attribute of God, and we'd take turns praising God. Then we'd sit quietly and let God speak to our hearts so we would know what sins we should confess to Him. Here, we took a short break from the regular Moms in Prayer format, and I would write down what each one felt God was telling them. This was a sweet yet powerful way to help them begin to listen for the promptings of the Holy Spirit. Then we would thank God for answered prayers and for our blessings. Lastly, we would lift our prayer requests up to God.

When I taught third and fourth grade Sunday school, I'd often incorporate parts of the four steps of prayer. What became obvious was that many kids felt uncomfortable praying out loud. To ease them into corporate prayer, I encouraged them to pray scriptures. I would give them a strip of paper with a printed scripture prayer with a space for them to write in their name or a friend's or relative's name. We'd break into smaller groups (which sometimes weren't that small), and take turns praying the scripture that was written in front of them. Those that felt comfortable would expand on their prayer. And those who were more nervous just read the prayer. What a powerful way to help kids become comfortable praying out loud!

Once a year, when we were in our big group of about 40 to 50, I'd share the story of God answering my daughter's very specific prayer request to illustrate that God will provide all our needs, but always in His perfect timing. When Zoe was in fifth grade, she begged and pleaded to have a dog that would snuggle with her in her bed. She prayed for the dog. She even wrote Santa asking for the dog for Christmas. I still have that letter that requested the dog be a dachshund, cuddly, and that would snuggle in her bed. We did look at our humane society occasionally, but the dogs she liked tended to have signs that read "not suitable for children."

God's perfect timing was a year later during Thanksgiving week. Zoe had had a year of horrible health issues, but the most prominent one at the time was CRPS that created a colorful, shiny bruise on her ankle. And, instead of healing, it kept screaming at her in pain. Horrifyingly, she went from being extremely active at the beginning of fifth grade to asking for a wheelchair in sixth grade. The rheumatologist explained that her brain wasn't sending signals that her ankle was healing. Instead, it was screaming, "This is the worst pain ever!" The rheumatologist and physical therapist both encouraged her to use the foot so the muscles wouldn't atrophy, even though it felt more natural to rest it. She started water therapy in a warm pool, but it was still too painful to walk very far. That is, until we found Red. He was exactly the dog she had prayed for a year ago. The day after we brought him home, Zoe wanted to be the first one to walk Red, so she walked around our neighborhood. To me, that was nothing short of a miracle—and all because we waited on God's timing.

Psalm 77:1-14

> I cried out to God for help;
>> I cried out to God to hear me.
> When I was in distress, I sought the Lord;
>> at night I stretched out untiring hands,
>> and I would not be comforted.
> I remembered you, God, and I groaned;
>> I meditated, and my spirit grew faint.
> You kept my eyes from closing;
>> I was too troubled to speak.
> I thought about the former days,
>> the years of long ago;
> I remembered my songs in the night.
>> My heart meditated and my spirit asked:
> "Will the Lord reject forever?
>> Will he never show his favor again?
> Has his unfailing love vanished forever?
>> Has his promise failed for all time?
> Has God forgotten to be merciful?
>> Has he in anger withheld his compassion?"
> Then I thought, "To this I will appeal:
>> the years when the Most High stretched out his right hand.
> I will remember the deeds of the LORD;
>> yes, I will remember your miracles of long ago.
> I will consider all your works
>> and meditate on all your mighty deeds."
> Your ways, God, are holy.
>> What god is as great as our God?
> You are the God who performs miracles;
>> you display your power among the peoples.

Several psalms encourage us again and again to "remember." Why? Because it's easy to forget. When there's an answer to prayer, tell your kids. When you see God's hand at work, tell your kids. Then, as you remember it—or as it shows back up in your social media history—remind your kids of God's faithfulness and how He answers prayers.

Another great way to bring your kids into prayer is to pray out loud immediately as the need arises. Maybe you're driving past an accident. Pray! Do you see a lost dog but can't stop to help? Pray it finds its way home. Does your child have a concern? Stop to pray with them. Let them see you pray with others, inviting Christ into a situation and asking that He answer according to His perfect plan and purpose. Then be sure to rejoice over the answers to prayer.

· ·

When there's an answer to prayer, tell your kids.
When you see God's hand at work, tell your kids.
Remind your kids of God's faithfulness
and how He answers prayers.

· ·

Nothing helps to develop a child's faith like seeing the living Christ answer our prayer requests in very specific ways—especially if it's a prayer request they have been praying for personally.

Help Kids Turn This World Upside Down for Christ

The disciples were going to turn this world upside down for Christ! To do so, they would need prayer. Our children also can turn this world around for Christ, so they too will need a prayer life. The disciples went to the right source: Jesus Himself.

Luke 11:1-4

It happened that while Jesus was praying in a certain place, after He had finished, one of His disciples said to Him, "Lord, teach us to pray just as John also taught his disciples."

And He said to them, "When you pray, say: 'Father, hallowed be Your name. Your kingdom come. Give us each day our daily bread. And forgive us our sins, For we ourselves also forgive everyone who is indebted to us. And lead us not into temptation'" (NASB).

Jesus not only taught His disciples how to pray, He taught them by example. In the verses that precede Luke 11:1-4 is an example of Mary and Martha. Martha was very busy serving the Lord and others. Can you see yourself in this story?

Luke 10:38-42

As Jesus and his disciples were on their way, he came to a village where a woman named Martha opened her home to him. She had a sister called Mary, who sat at the Lord's feet listening to what he said. But Martha was distracted by all the preparations that had to be made. She came to him and asked, "Lord, don't you care that my sister has left me to do the work by myself? Tell her to help me!"

"Martha, Martha," the Lord answered, "you are worried and upset about many things, but few things are needed— or indeed only one. Mary has chosen what is better, and it will not be taken away from her."

We can be so busy serving our family that we miss out on living a life of prayer! We see in the story that as Mary sat at Jesus's feet, that time spent would not be taken away from her. Whenever you take time to pray and sit at Jesus's feet by being in the Word, you will be transformed into His likeness! Prayer is an eternal work. I (Sally) learned to pray when I folded clothes or washed dishes. Or first thing in the morning, my family knew I was not to be disturbed for I was with Jesus. It is a hard battle to fight for that time, but the reward is eternal.

When Jesus was praying, God filled Him with power, peace, joy, and all He needed to do God's work. Prayer's transforming power empowered Jesus to endure all that was before Him. Jesus was extremely busy, but as He lived a life of prayer, His disciples saw its effects. I can only imagine what they saw on Jesus's face when He came back from His prayer time, because it was then that the disciples called out to Him to teach them to pray. And teach them He did! First He lived it, and then He shared it.

I believe we are always learning in prayer. Romans 8:26-27 says,

> In the same way the Spirit also helps our weakness; for we do not know how to pray as we should, but the Spirit Himself intercedes for us with groanings too deep for words; and He who searches the hearts knows what the mind of the Spirit is, because He intercedes for the saints according to the will of God (NASB).

The Holy Spirit is our resident teacher. And we will always grow in the realm of prayer if we practice it. Jesus gave the disciples a very simple outline to pray. In the first part of this book and in our other books—*Unshaken, Unshaken Study Guide*, and *Start with Praise*—you will see the same four prayer principles the Lord taught. The four simple, yet powerful steps we teach are praise, confession, thanksgiving, and intercession. Each step is life changing and keeps us focused on God.

Teach Children to Raise Up Others to the Lord

When my four children were young, I (Sally) had my daily time alone with God, and then they would come in my room, sit on my bed, and pray with me. Their ages ranged from one to 11 years old. We would read a scripture and sometimes a devotional. Then we would go through the four steps. When we got to intercession, we had lists of people to pray for each week. We would pray over teachers, relatives, siblings, etc., using God's Word. They were a little prayer army. And for anyone who didn't know Christ, we would pray using scriptures like Ephesians 1:13: "And you also were included in Christ when you heard the message of truth, the gospel of your salvation. When you believed, you were marked in him with a seal, the promised Holy Spirit." There were times when they would pray for a relative that was far away from God or a classmate growing up in a home without Christ. They would pray with great assurance that God would answer—and He did again and again.

> May _____ be included in Christ as he/she
> hears the message of truth, the gospel of his/her
> salvation, and believe so _____ will be marked
> in Him with a seal, the promised Holy Spirit.
>
> FROM EPHESIANS 1:13

Each week my youngest would pray for her second-grade friend, whose parents were Buddhist, to come with her to the after-school Good News Club. All year long her friend would say that she couldn't go. I was ready to give up, but not my daughter. Finally, on the last week, her friend went with her! Afterward, when I dropped the little girl off at home, her mom warmly greeted me, thanked me, and asked great questions about our faith—all because my daughter, her siblings, and I prayed. Many years later we are still seeing the prayed-for classmates coming to know Jesus. Our faith has grown through seeing the many answers to our prayers.

When my oldest was in high school, he was not a part of our time together because he joined his group of friends each morning at the high school flagpole to pray for the salvation of the students and teachers. Two of my children are part of their church prayer teams, using the same prayer steps they learned as a child.

Children have amazing faith. There is much we can teach them about prayer, and there is also much they will teach us through their trust in God and their faithfulness. Don't miss the chance to discover God's wonder and wisdom through the innocent and unwavering faith of a child.

Scripture Prayers for Teaching Kids to Pray

Lord, help me to train up my children in the
way they should go, so that even when they
are old they will not depart from it.

FROM PROVERBS 22:6 NASB

Lord, You are able to do immeasurably more than all we
ask or imagine, according to Your power that is at work
with us. To You be glory in the church and in Christ Jesus
throughout all generations, for ever and ever! Amen.

FROM EPHESIANS 3:20-21

Help my children know that as soon as we pray, You
answer us; You encourage us by giving us strength.

FROM PSALM 138:3 NLT

Oh Lord, may this be the cry of my children's hearts: "I
am praying to you because I know you will answer, O
God. Bend down and listen as I pray. Show me your
unfailing love in wonderful ways. By your mighty
power you rescue those who seek refuge from their
enemies. Guard me as you would guard your own
eyes. Hide me in the shadow of your wings."

PSALM 17:6-8 NLT

Lord, empower my children to know they are blessed if
they do not walk in step with the wicked or stand in the
way that sinners take or sit in the company of mockers,
but instead take delight in Your Word and meditate on
it day and night. Then they will be like trees planted by
streams of water, which yield their fruit in season and
whose leaves do not wither—whatever they do prospers.

FROM PSALM 1:1-3

Remind me to commend Your works to my children, to tell of Your mighty acts, to speak of the glorious splendor of Your majesty, and meditate on Your wonderful works. Help me not forget to tell of the power of Your awesome works and proclaim Your great deeds. May I always be an example of celebrating Your abundant goodness and joyfully singing of Your righteousness.

FROM PSALM 145:4-7

Lord, help me and my family keep Your commandments in our hearts. Help me impress them on my children. Remind me to talk about them when we sit at home and when we travel along the road, when they lie down for bed and when they get up.

FROM DEUTERONOMY 6:6-7

∽

Great is the LORD and most worthy of praise;
his greatness no one can fathom.
One generation commends your works to another;
they tell of your mighty acts.
They speak of the glorious splendor of your majesty—
and I will meditate on your wonderful works.
They tell of the power of your awesome works—
and I will proclaim your great deeds.
They celebrate your abundant goodness
and joyfully sing of your righteousness.
The LORD is gracious and compassionate,
slow to anger and rich in love.
The LORD is good to all;
he has compassion on all he has made.
All your works praise you, LORD;

your faithful people extol you.
They tell of the glory of your kingdom
and speak of your might,
so that all people may know of your mighty acts
and the glorious splendor of your kingdom.
Your kingdom is an everlasting kingdom,
and your dominion endures through all generations.
The LORD is trustworthy in all he promises
and faithful in all he does.

PSALM 145:3-13

17

The Power of Praying with Others

Again, truly I tell you that if two of you on
earth agree about anything they ask for,
it will be done for them by my Father in heaven.
For where two or three gather in my name, there am I with them.

MATTHEW 18:19-20

There were times when I (Sally) was so heavy with a burden for my child that when I came into our Moms in Prayer hour, I could only breathe a prayer. Have you ever been there? The weight is so heavy you cannot lift your arms in prayer. I hope this will encourage you.

Moses was to lead the children of Israel to the promised land so they could worship God. Whether you have one child or several children to mother, guide, and lift up, the role of mom can be so hard at times. Just imagine Moses having to lead over a million people to follow the Lord. God promised Moses—and us—that He will never leave him nor forsake him and that His presence would go with Moses. In Exodus 33:14-15, God said: "'My presence shall go with you, and I will give you rest.' Then he [Moses] said to Him, 'If Your presence does not go with us, do not lead us up from here'" (NASB). And yet we see Moses's arms growing tired as he was interceding for the children of Israel, who were in a battle.

Each day, our children are in a battle. How will we help them be victorious and reach the promised land? Read Exodus 17. The children of Israel were sent out to battle the enemy. Moses was stationed on top of the hill to intercede for them. He lifted his hands before the Lord. As long as his hands were raised up to the Lord, the children of Israel would win. Yet whenever his tired hands would come down, the enemy would win. His fellow servants of God joined him on behalf of the children of Israel. As it says in Exodus 17:12-13, "When Moses' hands grew tired, they took a stone and put it under him and he sat on it. Aaron and Hur held his hands up—one on one side, one on the other—so that his hands remained steady till sunset. So Joshua overcame the Amalekite army with the sword." Working together, they were victorious.

God gave Moses colaborers, just as He desires to give to you. They were stronger together than apart. God created us with a need for Him and others.

Ecclesiastes 4:9-12

> Two are better than one because they have a good return for their labor. For if either of them falls, the one will lift up his companion. But woe to the one who falls when there is not another to lift him up. Furthermore, if two lie down together they keep warm, but how can one be warm alone? And if one can overpower him who is alone, two can resist him. A cord of three strands is not quickly torn apart (NASB).

Why Two Are Better Than One

I am grateful when I think about how many times the women around me have lifted my arms up in prayer and helped my children through tough times. There were times when they would pray God's Word over my child, and I would, with a mustard seed of faith, touch their hands and only say, "I agree in Jesus's name, Amen."

Romans 8:26-27

> Likewise the Spirit also helps in our weaknesses. For we do not know what we should pray for as we ought, but the Spirit Himself makes intercession for us with groanings which cannot be uttered. Now He who searches the hearts knows what the mind of the Spirit is, because He makes intercession for the saints according to the will of God (NKJV).

Jackie Marcum tells a beautiful testimony of why two are better than one in prayer.

We have all been there. So overwhelmed by our circumstances that we can't find the words to cry out to God. I, for one, am so glad that we don't have to depend on our own words when we cry out to God. He knows our hearts, and the Holy Spirit intercedes on our behalf with "groanings" that cannot be confined by an earthly language. What a beautiful picture of God's deep love for us.

I have seen glimpses into what this looks like when my sisters in Christ lift up my children in our Moms in Prayer group. And never has there been a time when that picture was so vividly painted for me than when I went through a season when I was too heartbroken to pray.

On Christmas Eve in 2006, my beautiful, 6 year old niece Jenna went to be with Jesus after a valiant battle with a brain tumor. Over those 18 months, I cried out daily for God's healing hand to take away the tumor, and I knew He absolutely had the power to heal. When she died, my faith was shaken; it was hard to understand why God hadn't healed her here on this earth. But I knew my faithful God loved her more than I could ever imagine, and that is what got me through my grief.

After Christmas break, our Moms in Prayer group resumed

their weekly meetings, and I knew I needed to be there. My boys desperately needed prayers; they were all processing their grief in different ways, and it wasn't an easy road. But when I tried to lift them up in prayer, the tears began to flow, and I couldn't form the words to intercede on their behalf.

That is where my sisters in Christ took over. With the Holy Spirit guiding them, they lifted up my boys in prayer. The amazing thing is that they knew exactly how to pray for each one of them. The Holy Spirit not only knew what was on my heart, He knew what my children needed the most, and that is how the ladies in my Moms in Prayer group interceded for them. For months, these dear ladies would simply ask, "Who are we praying for today?" Sometimes, it was for one of my boys, and sometimes it was for one of Jenna's siblings. Then over time, these ladies helped me find the strength to pray out loud again. I truly don't know what I would have done without these precious prayer warriors in my life.

Now every week, I go to my Moms in Prayer group with great expectation. The Holy Spirit has already gone before the meeting, giving my group leader a Scripture verse that one of my boys desperately needs prayed over them. I pour out my heart on their behalf, and then I listen as the Spirit moves. My fellow prayer warrior prays in agreement for my son, and then she prays for things I didn't mention in my prayer. After she finishes, I can't help but think, "Why didn't I think about that? That is exactly what he needs right now." And then I just smile. I don't have to come up with the perfect words; the Holy Spirit intercedes for our children according to the will of the Father.

· ·

God created us with a need for Him and others.

· ·

Praying for Glimpses of God's Goodness

We never want to miss a week at our Moms in Prayer groups because we rejoice with each other when we see the prodigal come home, the disease healed, good grades achieved. We carry each other when life hurts beyond words, and when we want our children to see God's love in their lives. The other person you are praying with has an eternal, Holy Spirit gift for your child as you pray together. Don't go alone. Invite others to pray with you!

Let's share a few more stories. This one's from Christina Watson Manahan.

My daughter was on the varsity cheerleading squad, and unfortunately, the experience was not good for her. The main problem was that everyone was mean. The girls were not nice, and the coaches were not helpful. In fact, they seemed to make it worse. One day during our hour of Moms in Prayer, I got bold with my agreement of prayer for my daughter. All moms want their children to be happy and safe, and something needed to budge. I asked our Father to surprise my daughter with a wonderful day of smiles. "Father, everywhere she goes today, let people smile at her." I went on, "Let everyone smile at her: the girls on her squad, in school, and even the coaches to smile at her. And, Father, let it be so much smiling that she notices and wonders, 'Why is everyone smiling at me?'" My Moms in Prayer sister then prayed in agreement with me: "The LORD bless you and keep you; the LORD make His face shine on you and be gracious to you; the LORD turn his face toward you and give you peace" (Numbers 6:24-26).

Lord, bless _____ and keep him/her. Make Your face shine on _____ and be gracious to _____. Turn Your face toward _____ and give him/her peace.

FROM NUMBERS 6:24-26

What I am about to tell you should be the norm, and we shouldn't be surprised a bit. On that day when my daughter came home, she said, "Mom, it was so weird today at school. Everyone was smiling at me." She continued, "It was strange. Everywhere I went, they were smiling at me." I almost fell to my knees and was overcome with joy. God is so incredibly faithful; we just need to be bold enough to believe. The Bible tells us in James 4:2 that we have not because we ask not. He desires that we ask so that our joy may be full!

Praying While in the Belly of the Whale

Here's another testimony—this one from a British "mum."

I don't know about you, but I often find that people share testimonies of the great things God has done, and we rejoice with them, but then it can be easy to turn away and think, "But what about me, Lord? I am still in the belly of the whale!" Parenting, it seems to me, is a lifelong commitment.

Heartache and dashed hopes can seem to last forever too as we wait on the Lord's answers that so often do not come within our own chosen time frame. While pondering this, it occurred to me that Jonah didn't wait until he landed on the shore to praise God, but Jonah praised Him from the belly of the whale.

> I cried out to the LORD because of my affliction, And He answered me. Out of the belly of Sheol I cried, and You heard my voice...When my soul fainted within me, I remembered the LORD; and my prayer went up to You, into Your holy temple...But I will sacrifice to You with the voice of thanksgiving; I will pay what I have vowed. Salvation is of the LORD (Jonah 2:1-2,7,9 NKJV).

So, for those mums out there who, like me, might still be

there in the whale, I wanted to share some praise, as I know that God is with me and one day, because of His faithfulness, I shall yet see dry land. One way I know that He cares about me and my children so much is the way He brought Mums in Prayer into my life.

My husband and I met on the mission field in northern Asia, and on our wedding day, just after we made our vows and turned to walk down the aisle, someone leapt in front of us and said, "When your son is born, you shall call him..." Well, not an everyday occurrence! The name was an apostolic name, one I shall keep secret for my son's sake, but let's just say it spoke of the humble, godly character and missionary zeal we could anticipate in him. In due course, when I was still carrying him, I was given the same prophetic word while on two different continents—that my child would be greatly used of the Lord. I imagined him to be a contemporary John the Baptist, prophesying before he could walk. He did make a commitment to the Lord when he was young, but it took some years for me to realize that the reason that the Lord gave me these words was not because the fulfilment would be manifested from an early age, but because at times it would seem impossible to even imagine that this could come true.

Fifteen years ago, when the boys were very small, I came across a flyer about Mums in Prayer. A little while before that, a lady had joined our church. I introduced myself to this mother of six children, including a set of triplets, two of whom had special needs. We became friends, and I spoke to her about starting a Mums in Prayer group together. She wanted to, but sadly, the matter was dropped.

The years passed, and both of my sons were attending church with us and professing their own faith. Then came the hormones. Sound familiar? Teenage rebellion presented itself most strongly in our oldest son. Finally, one Sunday morning those heart-crushing words rang in my ears: "I'm not going to church, mum. I'm not a Christian anymore." What followed was a period in which our darling boy began experimenting with drugs and alcohol, started to drop out of school, and got into a cycle of extreme anxiety and depression that culminated in a complete breakdown with him being set back not one, but two years in his education.

In fall of 2014, to my complete surprise, I received a letter from our local Mums in Prayer area coordinator inviting me to a prayer breakfast. I'll be honest, my first thought was, "I haven't got time for that." Having delayed responding, I finally picked up the phone to politely decline, and within seconds of speaking to this lovely lady, I was in tears, pouring out my heart about my son. By 1:30 that afternoon, I was in a Mums in Prayer group. When God decides it is time for something, there's no arguing.

By Christmas, we began to see the first signs of answered prayer. We discovered a whole series of laptop tabs open to You-Tube videos about end-times and other Christian themes. Previously, the Lord had spoken to me very clearly from Joshua 6:10 to "not...let a word proceed out of your mouth, until the day I tell you" (NASB). I had to keep quiet and let God do it. However, there have been moments of grace. Our son has begun to ask questions, and I even found myself sitting up with him at one in the morning discussing end-times, God, and faith. Although not yet walking with the Lord, he has, I would say, aligned himself with Christians and is again beginning to show that he believes.

Having attended the Mums in Prayer group for almost a year, I began to sense it was time to set up a more local group. I contacted my friend, the mother of six, and reminded her of Mums in Prayer. We hadn't attended the same church in a long time, and, as busy working mums, we had been trying to get together for coffee, without success. Yet, we found that, because of the focused hour of power prayer arrangement of MIPI, we were able to meet and pray every week without fail. Also, the Lord has been bringing other mums, and we are now a group of five. It's a priceless blessing to sit with other mums, sharing tears, pain, and burdens, but also hope, encouragement, and love. It is also a great honor and privilege to bring hope to other mums who are desperate to see the power of God's intervention in their own child's life through prayer.

As for our son? He is now nearly 20 and, having been told he was in the top quartile in his year, with every expectation of academic success, and with just a handful of classes left, he has dropped out of education altogether for the moment. Feeling unable to face the stress, he tells me, "I'll be a street cleaner; it's all I'm worth." As only God can do, a "chance remark" at our Mums in Prayer group the preceding week led us to an agency (run by a Christian!) which offers sheltered housing to young people who are struggling and supports them into employment, apprenticeships, or education and towards independence. This looks to be the next step that the Lord has for him.

I had been worried that my son was angry with God because he suffers so much with his health; he's in constant pain, he cannot sleep, and he's often nauseated. When my Mums in Prayer group met, my intercessory prayer for him was that he would not be mad at God. That evening, I told him I would understand if he was angry with God because of his difficulties. He interrupted me and said, "I am not angry with God. I am angry, but not with God. It is not His fault. He didn't do this to me." I nearly wept. Praise the Lord! He answered that prayer within hours of my request. It gave me so much more peace about a reconciliation between my son and God.

My son is an unfinished work, and I will have to let him go. But I have the peace of mind that the Lord has His hand on him, and though the vision tarry, it will surely come, and I have the comfort of my MIP group to help pray for it. Just this week, he has been ill. Lying in bed, with his face to the wall, for the first time in so many years he asked me, "Mum, please, will you pray for me?" Oh yes, my darling. And I will never stop.

How God Transformed a "Worst Day"

Allow us to share one more story of the power of praying with others. This one is from Margaret Haire.

Let me tell you about the worst day in my life. It was November 7, 2006. My son had a huge disappointment after years of working toward and sacrificing for something that was supposed to come to fruition on that day. My daughter was a freshman in college and had just broken off a very special relationship with a young man she had known for many years. She called to tell me about that and also shared she had spoken to a counselor who told her she was becoming anorexic in response to the end of this longtime friendship.

On this same day, November 7, 2006, I had to put our beloved 16-year-old dog, Buster, to sleep. All of these things were so grievous for me, I couldn't sleep. After tossing and turning for hours, I got up around 3 a.m. and emailed my friend and asked her to pray. My friend and I had been praying together since our daughters were in grade school. She prayed throughout the morning for my family, and our scheduled prayer time was that afternoon, the hour before school let out. When we met up that afternoon, we began with Psalm 84 as a springboard to praise and adoration:

> How lovely is your dwelling place,
>   LORD Almighty!
> My soul yearns, even faints,
>   for the courts of the LORD;

my heart and my flesh cry out
   for the living God.
Even the sparrow has found a home,
   and the swallow a nest for herself,
   where she may have her young—
a place near your altar,
   Lord Almighty, my King and my God.
Blessed are those who dwell in your house;
   they are ever praising you.
Blessed are those whose strength is in you,
   whose hearts are set on pilgrimage.
As they pass through the Valley of Baka,
   they make it a place of springs;
   the autumn rains also cover it with pools.
They go from strength to strength,
   till each appears before God in Zion.
Hear my prayer, Lord God Almighty;
   listen to me, God of Jacob.
Look on our shield, O God;
   look with favor on your anointed one.
Better is one day in your courts
   than a thousand elsewhere;
I would rather be a doorkeeper in the house of my God
   than dwell in the tents of the wicked.
For the Lord God is a sun and shield;
   the Lord bestows favor and honor;
no good thing does he withhold
   from those whose walk is blameless.
Lord Almighty,
   blessed is the one who trusts in you.

Verse 3 says, "Even the sparrow has found a home and the swallow a nest for herself, where she may have her young—a place near your altar." When we finished reading the psalm, my friend looked up and said, "Margaret, unbelievably this random hymn, 'His Eye Is on the Sparrow,' has been running through my head all morning as I was praying for your daughter." We looked at each other and shook our heads and, with tears in our eyes, both said this felt like a confirmation from God. It was as if God was saying, "Hey, I've got this! My eye is on your little sparrow. She has a nest near My altar; she has a place in My home, and it's a home where she is safe with Me. What she needs to do, and what you need to do, is to come to Me, come dwell inside My house, praising and trusting Me. In My house there is safety, protection, strength, blessings, and peace. It is a place where your children will grow strong, and where they will become a blessing to others. When they set their hearts on knowing Me, I will take them from strength to strength, and bestow upon them favor and honor."

November 7, 2006, was the worst day in my life because a mother loves her children with such intensity that our hearts break when our children's hearts break. But what does the psalmist say? He says as our children who are seeking to know God go through the places of deep sorrow, God strengthens them and makes the valley places into places of renewal and refreshment. God is so good that He leads them out of the valleys. He helps them turn their sorrows into blessings, their tears into fountains of renewal, their sad times into springs of refreshment and restoration not just for themselves but for others.

That's what my friend did for me. She had gone through the valley of deep sorrows with her heart breaking as she watched her daughter go deeper into the nightmare that is anorexia. For a while, she carried this heavy burden by herself. After all, she had dedicated her life to her children. She gave up her career to raise them. She brought them up in the church. She sent them to a Christian school. She was a great mother. But her beautiful, very smart, incredibly talented and gifted daughter was starving herself to death. For a while, out of embarrassment, out of a desire for privacy, and even out of a sense of shame, my friend carried this burden alone. But the load became too much to bear, and she shared it with others, including me, her prayer partner in our Moms in Prayer group. She shared it with a family member who prayed intensely for her daughter. Yes, she and her husband took practical steps to intervene and to help their daughter, but the turning point came when the family member cried out to God on behalf of her daughter. It was the power of the Holy Spirit working through prayer that ultimately delivered her out of anorexia.

And now this mom, my prayer partner, was praying for my daughter's path. My friend was helping me and my daughter in the same way that she and her daughter had been helped. She was helping me carry the heavy load of a broken heart, and she was walking with me in the valley of sorrow by lifting my daughter in prayer.

That's what Moms in Prayer and praying in one accord is all about. No matter how competent and confident we might be, we still need each other. All of us have times when we don't feel very strong. So often young moms feel lonely—or at least all alone—in raising their children. In coming together to lift up our children and each other's children to Jesus, God strengthens us, and He binds our hearts together.

Sometimes it truly is a lifeline, especially during the times when we feel like we're drowning. Other times we experience the great joy of throwing a lifeline to our praying sisters when they are overwhelmed and drowning in the valley of sorrows. Watching them lift their eyes away from their troubles and look up for help is so rewarding and encouraging. Pushing aside embarrassment and desires for privacy and allowing a trusted sister to pray for you and your children is such a blessing. What a gift to us when someone else lifts our families to Christ. What joy it is to see how God answers our prayers!

He certainly said yes to our prayers for my daughter and my

son. They are both grown and doing well with families of their own. I continue to pray for them and for my grandchildren, as well as for the children and grandchildren of my dear friends in our Moms in Prayer group—over 20 years of praying! God alone knows how He has answered all of those prayers. But I do know that God answers prayer, and that my Moms in Prayer group has been a lifesaver for me. It's one of the best child-rearing things I have ever done! Life has its best days, life has its worst days, and life has its ordinary days. But every day we need God, and our families need God. When we cry out to Him in prayer, we all will find our strength, our joy, our ability to help others. We and our families will gain our sense of home, identity, and purpose. As the last line of Psalm 84 says, "LORD Almighty, blessed is the one who trusts in you!"

* *

Life has its best days, life has its worst days, and life has its ordinary days. But every day we need God.

* *

Scripture Prayers
for Finding Prayer Partners

Lord, Matthew 18:19-20 says, "Truly I tell you that if two of you on earth agree about anything they ask for, it will be done for them by my Father in heaven. For where two or three gather in my name, there am I with them." Lord, help me find at least one other person with whom I can gather in Your name and pray on a regular basis.

As Moses had in Exodus 17:12-13, help me, Lord, to find prayer partners who can come alongside me and help me seek Your strength and power when I grow weary.

Lord, help me to grow my faith that's the size of a mustard seed so I can say to this mountain, "Move from here to there," and trust that it will move because nothing is impossible with You.

FROM MATTHEW 17:20

Lord, You tell us in James 4:2, "You do not have because you do not ask God." Help me to always remember to bring my cares and concerns to You and to ask You for help.

Help me live this out in front of my children and others: May I never be lacking in zeal, but keep my spiritual fervor, serving the Lord. Empower me to be joyful in hope, patient in affliction, faithful in prayer.

FROM ROMANS 12:11-12

Oh Lord, help me find someone who can join me in following the call for intercession for our children in Lamentations 2:19: "Arise, cry out in the night, as the watches of the night begin; pour out your heart like water in the presence of the Lord. Lift

up your hands to him for the lives of your children,
who faint from hunger at every street corner."

∽

Therefore, I urge you, brothers and sisters,
in view of God's mercy,
to offer your bodies as a living sacrifice,
holy and pleasing to God—
this is your true and proper worship.
Do not conform to the pattern of this world,
but be transformed by the renewing of your mind.
Then you will be able to test
and approve what God's will is—his
good, pleasing and perfect will.

Romans 12:1-2

18

Continuing to Pray God's Word

I keep my eyes always on the LORD. With him
at my right hand, I will not be shaken.

PSALM 16:8

Just because you're nearing the final sentence in this book doesn't mean the scripture prayers have ended. No matter which of life's twists and turns come your way, keep praying. When we keep our eyes focused on the Lord, He will help us withstand whatever comes our way. Maintaining our focus on Jesus Christ as our Lord and Savior will empower us to stand boldly and unshaken. Consider these verses:

> Since, then, you have been raised with Christ, set your hearts on things above, where Christ is, seated at the right hand of God. Set your minds on things above, not on earthly things (Colossians 3:1-2).
> But seek first his kingdom and his righteousness, and all these things will be given to you as well (Matthew 6:33).
> I keep my eyes always on the LORD. With him at my right hand, I will not be shaken (Psalm 16:8).

For me (Cyndie) my greatest joy in the morning is sitting down in my cozy, red quiet-time chair, opening my well-worn Bible, and reading, meditating on, and praying through the Scriptures. Starting my day off with the Lord allows me to "seek first his kingdom and his righteousness." It better enables me to set my heart and mind on Christ so I can aim to stand firm, no matter what the day brings. Often a passage will jump off the page and hit me exactly where I am at that moment, and it feels like a special gift straight from heaven. I meditate on the passage, reflecting on what it means and how I can apply it to my own life. Is there an attribute of God that I can praise Him for? Is there something convicting in this passage that I need to confess? What do I need to remember to be thankful for? And to whom does this verse apply? I typically pray it for myself, my family, and whomever God places on my heart. If I'm going on the elliptical or a walk afterward, I'll usually take a picture of the passage and continue meditating on it and praying through it while I'm exercising, and then as I go throughout the day.

Our encouragement to you is to carve out some daily time to spend with the Lord. Start with reading God's Word—whether with a traditional paper version of the Bible, or a digital or audio version. If spending daily time in the Word isn't part of your routine yet, consider starting with the daily Scripture that YouVersion offers with push notification. Whatever scripture you're reading, take a moment and ask the Lord to show you what it means and how you can apply it to your life. Then pray through the four steps of prayer: praise, confession, thanksgiving, and intercession. Of course, in your personal quiet time, it is always appropriate to pray for yourself as well!

Enjoy a Quiet Time with the Steps of Prayer

- *Praise:* Is there an attribute of God demonstrated in the passage, or is there a characteristic of God that you're reminded of? Take time to start by praising God for who He is.

- *Confession:* Is there something in the scripture that's convicting, that you feel the Holy Spirit nudging you to confess? Don't hang on to it. If you do, God will just keep bringing it back up. Stop at that moment and repent of the sin, and ask God to help you improve in that area. Remember, God never expects us to do anything in our own strength—including confession. Ask Him to help you, and He will!

- *Thanksgiving:* Spend time thanking the Lord for what you see in that scripture, as well as your blessings and how God is working in your life. Focusing on gratitude can transform our minds, so start the day with a thankful heart.

- *Intercession:* Ask God to help you know for whom you should pray the scripture that you're reading. As He brings each person to mind, allow the Holy Spirit to prompt your prayers, praying the scripture and then praying specifically as the Spirit leads. Don't feel that you have to finish praying during your official "quiet time." Use your phone to take a screen shot or photo of the verse and carry it with you during the day, praying for different people as the Holy Spirit directs you. Remember, when we pray God's Word, we know we are praying God's will!

- *Petition:* Of course, in your quiet time, it's always okay to pray the scripture for yourself! Allow the beauty and power of God's Word to penetrate your heart and your mind. Wrap up in God's holy Word as if you're wrapping up in your favorite blanket. Let it provide protection and warmth from the world and stressors that await. Spend time asking God how you can live out the Scripture verses that He's given you today, despite what comes. Remember Psalm 16:8: If we keep our eyes on the Lord throughout the day, we will not be shaken.

Diving into God's Word for Scripture Prayers

When my heart is heavy and my prayer list is long, I'll often turn to the Psalms and meditate on a passage one section at a time. Don't feel like you have to race through your Bible reading. If the Holy Spirit nudges you on a verse, stop and meditate on it, thinking about what it means and praying the passage for you and a loved one. Additionally, the Proverbs offer plenty of scriptures to pray over our kids. With 31 chapters, it's a perfect book to read one chapter at a time for a month to help you develop the joy and habit of praying through God's Word. But don't feel you need to race through your time with God. If He has you lingering over a verse or section, stay there. Sometimes I go back to the same passage several days in a row to meditate on it and pray through it.

If you're reading this book with your spouse, start praying scripture prayers for your kids together. Or grab a friend and begin praying. Looking for a prayer partner? In the next chapter, Sally talks about our Moms in Prayer groups and how to either find or start one.

We appreciate you joining us on this journey of praying scriptures for our kids. We'll end our time together with some great scriptures to meditate on and pray for your children. We'll offer some from the Psalms, a sampling of Paul's prayers—which make great jumping-off points for praying scriptures—and a few from Proverbs.

Psalm 1:1-3

> Blessed is the one
>   who does not walk in step with the wicked
> or stand in the way that sinners take
>   or sit in the company of mockers,
> but whose delight is in the law of the LORD,
>   and who meditates on his law day and night.
> That person is like a tree planted by streams of water,
>   which yields its fruit in season

and whose leaf does not wither—
whatever they do prospers.

Psalm 37:23-24,39-40 NLT

The Lord directs the steps of the godly.
He delights in every detail of their lives.
Though they stumble, they will never fall,
for the LORD holds them by the hand...

The LORD rescues the godly;
he is their fortress in times of trouble.
The LORD helps them,
rescuing them from the wicked.
He saves them,
and they find shelter in him.

Philemon 1:4-7

I always thank my God as I remember you in my prayers,
because I hear about your love for all his holy people and
your faith in the Lord Jesus. I pray that your partnership
with us in the faith may be effective in deepening your
understanding of every good thing we share for the sake
of Christ. Your love has given me great joy and encouragement, because you, brother, have refreshed the hearts of
the Lord's people.

Colossians 1:3-6,7-14

We always thank God, the Father of our Lord Jesus Christ,
when we pray for you, because we have heard of your faith
in Christ Jesus and of the love you have for all God's people—the faith and love that spring from the hope stored
up for you in heaven and about which you have already
heard in the true message of the gospel that has come to

you. In the same way, the gospel is bearing fruit and growing throughout the whole world—just as it has been doing among you since the day you heard it and truly understood God's grace…For this reason, since the day we heard about you, we have not stopped praying for you. We continually ask God to fill you with the knowledge of his will through all the wisdom and understanding that the Spirit gives, so that you may live a life worthy of the Lord and please him in every way: bearing fruit in every good work, growing in the knowledge of God, being strengthened with all power according to his glorious might so that you may have great endurance and patience, and giving joyful thanks to the Father, who has qualified you to share in the inheritance of his holy people in the kingdom of light. For he has rescued us from the dominion of darkness and brought us into the kingdom of the Son he loves, in whom we have redemption, the forgiveness of sins.

Ephesians 1:15-18

For this reason, ever since I heard about your faith in the Lord Jesus and your love for all God's people, I have not stopped giving thanks for you, remembering you in my prayers. I keep asking that the God of our Lord Jesus Christ, the glorious Father, may give you the Spirit of wisdom and revelation, so that you may know him better. I pray that the eyes of your heart may be enlightened in order that you may know the hope to which he has called you, the riches of his glorious inheritance in his holy people,

Proverbs 1:1-10 NLT

These are the proverbs of Solomon, David's son, king of Israel.
Their purpose is to teach people wisdom and discipline,
    to help them understand the insights of the wise.
Their purpose is to teach people to live disciplined and

successful lives,
    to help them do what is right, just, and fair.
These proverbs will give insight to the simple,
    knowledge and discernment to the young.
Let the wise listen to these proverbs and become even wiser.
    Let those with understanding receive guidance
by exploring the meaning in these proverbs and parables,
    the words of the wise and their riddles.
Fear of the LORD is the foundation of true knowledge,
    but fools despise wisdom and discipline.
My child, listen when your father corrects you.
    Don't neglect your mother's instruction.
What you learn from them will crown you with grace
    and be a chain of honor around your neck.
My child, if sinners entice you,
    turn your back on them!

Proverbs 10:8-12,17-21,23-26

The wise in heart accept commands,
    but a chattering fool comes to ruin.
Whoever walks in integrity walks securely,
    but whoever takes crooked paths will be found out.
Whoever winks maliciously causes grief,
    and a chattering fool comes to ruin.
The mouth of the righteous is a fountain of life,
    but the mouth of the wicked conceals violence.
Hatred stirs up conflict,
    but love covers over all wrongs...

Whoever heeds discipline shows the way to life,
    but whoever ignores correction leads others astray.
Whoever conceals hatred with lying lips
    and spreads slander is a fool.
Sin is not ended by multiplying words,
    but the prudent hold their tongues.

The tongue of the righteous is choice silver,
    but the heart of the wicked is of little value.
The lips of the righteous nourish many,
    but fools die for lack of sense...

A fool finds pleasure in wicked schemes,
    but a person of understanding delights in wisdom.
What the wicked dread will overtake them;
    what the righteous desire will be granted.
When the storm has swept by, the wicked are gone,
    but the righteous stand firm forever.
As vinegar to the teeth and smoke to the eyes,
    so are sluggards to those who send them.

Proverbs 11:2-6,12-13,25-27

When pride comes, then comes disgrace,
    but with humility comes wisdom.
The integrity of the upright guides them,
    but the unfaithful are destroyed by their duplicity.
Wealth is worthless in the day of wrath,
    but righteousness delivers from death.
The righteousness of the blameless makes their paths straight,
    but the wicked are brought down by their own wickedness.
The righteousness of the upright delivers them,
    but the unfaithful are trapped by evil desires...

Whoever derides their neighbor has no sense,
    but the one who has understanding holds their tongue.
A gossip betrays a confidence,
    but a trustworthy person keeps a secret...

A generous person will prosper;
    whoever refreshes others will be refreshed.
People curse the one who hoards grain,

but they pray God's blessing on the one who is
willing to sell.
Whoever seeks good finds favor,
but evil comes to one who searches for it.

Proverbs 14:16-17,29

The wise fear the LORD and shun evil,
but a fool is hotheaded and yet feels secure.
A quick-tempered person does foolish things,
and the one who devises evil schemes is hated...

Whoever is patient has great understanding,
but one who is quick-tempered displays folly.

Proverbs 16:1-9

To humans belong the plans of the heart,
but from the LORD comes the proper answer of the tongue.
All a person's ways seem pure to them,
but motives are weighed by the LORD.
Commit to the LORD whatever you do,
and he will establish your plans.
The LORD works out everything to its proper end—
even the wicked for a day of disaster.
The LORD detests all the proud of heart.
Be sure of this: They will not go unpunished.
Through love and faithfulness sin is atoned for;
through the fear of the LORD evil is avoided.
When the LORD takes pleasure in anyone's way,
he causes their enemies to make peace with them.
Better a little with righteousness
than much gain with injustice.
In their hearts humans plan their course,
but the LORD establishes their steps.

A Personal Invitation from Sally to Moms of All Ages

What if you could change the world not just for today but for generations to come? At Moms in Prayer International, we believe that lives and whole communities are changed forever when we gather together to pray to the only One who can change a human heart. We can make the difference as we reach out to God in prayer.

As you prayed for your loved ones through this book, you touched heaven on their behalf. We want to give you the opportunity to take your prayer life to the next level by praying with others. There is great power in unified prayer. When I (Sally) joined Moms in Prayer International, I had never prayed out loud before, and today I now equip, empower, and encourage women all over the world to pray. What will God do through you and your loved ones as you pray alongside others?

If you're a mom, grandma, aunt, or woman concerned with the next generation, we encourage you to join a Moms in Prayer group. Praying the four steps of prayer—praise, silent confession, thanksgiving, and intercession—alongside another woman on behalf of your children is a powerful way to bring your burdens to the Lord. We have seen God transform lives in mighty ways as women come together to pray for children, their schools, and the school staff.

As president of Moms in Prayer International, I want to personally invite you to join us. Moms in Prayer happens when two or more women gather together one hour weekly and pray for children and schools. As they pray, they are impacting children and schools for Christ! There is a group in your area waiting for you to join them—or waiting for you to start a group!

We currently have Moms in Prayer groups in every state in the USA and in over 140 countries worldwide. We are women with children/grandchildren/loved ones in a variety of schools—public, private, charter, homeschool, preschool, college—and some pray for grown children and adopt a school to pray for.

Our vision is that every school in the world will be covered in prayer so every child will be prayed for. The children and schools of the world are in great need of our prayers. It is a God-sized vision, and God is leading us forward.

Fern Nichols started Moms in Prayer International in 1984 when she cried out to God to bring her at least one other mom to pray with her for her two eldest sons and their junior high school. God brought her more than just one other mom! Since then, Moms in Prayer International has become a prayer movement impacting thousands of children and schools each year. Wherever there is a Moms in Prayer group, we see revival and spiritual awakening happening. We have witnessed families, schools, villages, towns, cities, and countries transformed for Christ as we pray.

God has great plans for the children of the world, no matter their age. So we must be praying for them. Come join us, and I promise God will bless you beyond measure!

JOIN MOMS IN PRAYER

For more information, visit www.MomsInPrayer.org. Start by checking to see if there's a group near you. If not, the website offers all the resources you need to start a group. By registering your group online, your local Moms in Prayer leadership will offer you support as you begin. If you need additional assistance finding or starting a group, please contact info@MomsInPrayer.org or call (855) 769-7729.

SIGN UP FOR SCRIPTURE PRAYER EMAILS

While our prayer groups are designed for women, we invite everyone to sign up for our scripture prayers, which are emailed Monday through Friday. Register at www.MomsInPrayer.org, where you'll find many other resources to help you continue to pray scriptures for your children.

KEEP PRAYING!

What a privilege it has been to have you join us on this journey of prayer. Thank you for praying for this next generation, using the power of God's Word.

Our hope and prayer is that this book will be one that you turn to as your children grow through their various stages. Maybe you'll have a favorite scripture that you'll pray over your child throughout his/her life. Or maybe different scriptures will be the cry of your heart, depending on the character-shaping challenges your child is facing. In any case, dear readers, please know that we pray that God will use this book to help you pray God's words into the lives of the children in your life.

We finish our time together just as we started: with a scripture prayer for you:

> *May the LORD answer you when you are in distress;*
> *may the name of the God of Jacob protect you.*
> *May he send you help from the sanctuary*
> *and grant you support...*
> *May he give you the desire of your heart*
> *and make all your plans succeed.*
> *May we shout for joy over your victory*
> *and lift up our banners in the name of our God.*

PSALM 20:1-2,4-5

About Sally

Sally Burke, president of Moms in Prayer International, grew up in Cocoa Beach, Florida. As a girl, she was fascinated with the space program and later became a space shuttle engineer. She has her master's of science degree, but it is the Word of God that has her heart now. It wasn't until after she married and gave birth to her first two children that she and her husband came to faith in Christ, and God changed her priorities. Her introduction to Moms in Prayer International in 1990 was life changing. As a young mom and a new believer, she discovered how faithfully God works in kids' lives in answer to prayer, and she experienced the powerful bond of sisterhood among praying moms. Sally began to share this hope with others.

In 2008, Sally "took on the world" for Moms in Prayer International as the director of field ministry, providing spiritual and strategic direction to the ministry worldwide. During her tenure, God doubled the number of nations where Moms in Prayer groups are found.

Today, in her role as president of Moms in Prayer International, Sally is carrying on the legacy begun in 1984. The coauthor of *Unshaken, Unshaken Study Guide*, and *Start with Praise*, Sally is a dynamic speaker and teacher who loves to encourage, equip, and empower women around the world in prayer. She has been a guest on James Dobson's national radio program *Family Talk* as well as on *Today's Faith*, Calvary Chapel's national broadcast, and many other international, national, and regional programs, podcasts, and webinars, and at churches, retreats, Bible studies, and gatherings around the world.

Sally and her husband, Ed, have four adult children—son Ryan (married to Claire), daughter Ginae (married to Garrett), son David (married to Liz), and daughter Aubrie—and three grandchildren: Grant, Genevieve, and Ella.

**To contact Sally,
email her at info@momsinprayer.org**

About Cyndie

Cyndie Claypool de Neve, a former journalist who has an M.A. in Counseling Psychology, is the author of *God-Confident Kids: Helping Your Child Find True Purpose, Passion and Peace*. Scheduled for release October 2019, this Baker Books offering encourages parents, teachers, coaches, and mentors to remind kids that each one was handcrafted by God, on purpose for a good purpose (Ephesians 2:10).

Passionate about prayer and helping children and adults discover their God-given purpose, Cyndie enjoys speaking and teaching, and has led many seminars, workshops, classes, events, Bible studies, and groups. She is the coauthor of the devotional *Start with Praise*, published by Harvest House in 2018, *Unshaken* and *Unshaken Study Guide*, published by Harvest House in 2017, and *When Moms Pray Together*, published by Tyndale House in 2009.

As the director of communications at Moms in Prayer International for five years, Cyndie launched the ministry's social media presence. To encourage moms to pray daily, she coordinated the creation of the daily scripture prayers, emailed to thousands of people every weekday morning. She also helped establish the church-wide day of prayer, Bless Our Schools Sunday.

Today, she works as the senior director of creative and technical services at Emmanuel Faith Community Church in Escondido, California. She leads a team of eight, overseeing communications, graphics, video, media, and IT, and enjoys her Sunday mornings as she welcomes visitors and helps them find ways to get connected at church.

Cyndie and her husband, Marcel, live in Escondido, California, with their two creative children—Elliott and Zoe—and two rambunctious rescue dogs.

To contact Cyndie,
visit www.cyndiedeneve.com

Unshaken

Your Faith Will Stand Unshaken When Your Prayers Shake Up the World

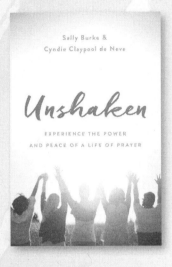

As you pray to the God of the universe, you're free to ask for the seemingly impossible. Align your heart with His will and pray with confidence, knowing He will answer according to His perfect plans and mighty power.

Join authors Sally Burke, president of Moms in Prayer International, and Cyndie Claypool de Neve on a quest to pray boldly in your daily struggles and difficult trials. When your strength is in short supply and your courage is battered, it's time to...

- Discover the power of a biblical four-step prayer process that defeats fear
- Read stories of women who experienced answered prayer in desperate circumstances
- Learn how to pray for yourself and your loved ones in accordance with God's will

Your family and future are in secure hands when you release them to Jesus. And as you pray with firm faith, you'll see yourself and your world transformed.

Unshaken Study Guide

I keep my eyes always on the LORD.
With him at my right hand,
I will not be shaken.

PSALM 16:8

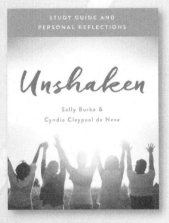

You have every reason to pray with confidence when you're praying to the God of the universe in accordance with His perfect will. Learn how to pray boldly and consistently in this companion guide to *Unshaken* by Sally Burke, president of Moms in Prayer International, and Cyndie Claypool de Neve.

With provocative questions, recommended Scripture reading, and inspiring activities to complete, you'll discover fresh insights into prayer and be encouraged to entrust your family and future into the secure hands of Jesus.

Dig deep into this all-important study with a group or on your own, and get ready to see yourself and your world transformed.

Start with Praise

Feeling Inadequate
Be Empowered!

Today's needs and tomorrow's uncertainties can bring us to our knees. We often don't feel up to the task of carrying out God's mission with strength and courage in our jobs, activities, and families.

Let this 40-day devotional help empower you to be bold in all you do and to experience the joys of faithful prayer. Just like Jesus chose 12 ordinary men to be His disciples, God placed *you* right where you are—in the middle of an ordinary life that can have eternal impact.

Follow the Moms in Prayer four-step prayer process day by day and learn how to invite God's power into every area of your heart. It all starts with praise...

∽